Early Photographs and Early Photographers

Early Photographs and Early Photographers

a Survey in Dictionary Form

by Oliver Mathews

Reedminster Publications Ltd.
23 Suffolk Road, London, S.W.13

First published by Reedminster Publications Ltd. 1973

ISBN 0 85945 001 5

All enquiries and requests relevant to this title should be sent to the publisher, Reedminster Publications Ltd., 23 Suffolk Road, London, S.W.13, and not to the printer.

Printed in England by Adlard & Son Ltd., Bartholomew Press, Dorking, Surrey

Contents

Acknowledgments

But for my wife, Sheila, this book would never have been completed. I thank her, not only for taking and making more than half of the copy photographs but especially for her ceaseless encouragement and wise advice.

Many friends have given valuable assistance along the way and I would like to thank in particular Mr. Otto Bettmann of the Bettmann Archives; Mrs. Gail Buckland of the Royal Photographic Society; Mr. Joe Coltharp of the Gernsheim Collection at the University of Texas; Mr. Christopher Hobbs of the Victoria & Albert Museum; Mlle de Jendin of the Bibliothèque Nationale; Mrs. Grace M. Mayer of the Museum of Modern Art; Mme Christiane Roger of the Société Française de Photographie; Mrs. Edna J. Williams of the University of Pennsylvania Library; Sampson Low, Marston, Searle & Rivington Ltd. (for permission to quote from *Naturalistic Photography* by Peter Henry Emerson); Mr. D. L. Day; Miss Catherine Pattison; and Mr. Ian Straker.

Finally, I acknowledge and thank the various institutions, bodies and collections who have kindly given permission for the reproduction of photographs in their care—a full list is to be found at the end of the text.

Introduction

The first photographs ever were taken during the 1820s. The daguerreotype process was published in 1839; the calotype in 1841. The wet plate process was introduced in 1851; the dry plate in 1871.

Nicéphore Niépce; William Henry Fox Talbot; David Octavius Hill and Robert Adamson; Mathew B. Brady; Nadar; Julia Margaret Cameron; Lewis Carroll; Frank Meadows Sutcliffe; Alfred Stieglitz.

The basic facts and the great names form the heart of this book. Descriptions of the various types of photography, minor incidents, some multifarious chemical processes and some less well known names form the body. The latter are very much a personal selection; seasoning a mixture of American, French and English photographers, with some Austrian names, some Japanese ones, an Irishman, a South African, two New Zealanders and so on, in an attempt to give a cross section, a survey, of early photographers. The inclusion of one name or the exclusion of another must not be taken as any measure of either fame or obscurity. Space forbids mention of every single person and occasion—there were so many thousands—and the aim here is to supply a general knowledge in reference form.

The illustrations have been chosen with similar thoughts. Several of the world's greatest and best known early photographs are included; several tried and trusted friends, some entirely new ones, some really beautiful photographs, some amusing ones and a few very sad ones; some via comparatively obscure cameras and sources, others from the traditional sources. In short, there are as many as possible; selected to serve as examples of specific photographers' work as well as sharpen the senses and excite the taste for the wonderful successes of early photography.

Chronologically the entries close somewhere between 1910 and 1914. By this time the various styles and processes in 'black and white' may be said to have run their first full cycle: from the early pioneering experiments involving simple representation, through the daguerreotypes, the calotypes, the wet plates and all the controlled print processes of the late nineteenth century and very early 1900s, returning to the straight, pure photography led largely by the 'American School' at the beginning of this century; whilst the widespread development and use of colour photography was still to come.

Finally, in the belief that a long overdue and popular interest in early photography is at last beginning to materialize, and that many of us cannot resist the temptation of acquisition, an exploratory guide to the current prices for early photographs is also included.

In all, I hope that this particular essay achieves a fairly fierce incision into the marvellous subject of early photographs and early photographers; furnishing the foremost facts and figures whilst whetting the appetite.

The Origins and Prehistory

The phenomenon of the camera obscura (literally a 'dark room'), whereby a small hole in the wall of a blacked out room or box will transmit the view outside to the opposite interior wall, has been well appreciated by wise and learned men for two and three thousand years.

Leonardo da Vinci (1450–1519), aware of everything scientific besides artistic, wrote accounts of the phenomenon some fifty years before the publication in 1558 of a detailed description of a camera obscura and its workings by the Neapolitan Giovanni Battista della Porta (1538–1615). Later in the sixteenth and seventeenth centuries the lens became a desirable addition and the apparatus itself a frequent aid to artists. Improved lenses, mirror reflexes and, most important, reduction of size—from that of a room to a quite small box—followed and continued through the eighteenth and early nineteenth centuries leading to one of the most delightful of all understatements of all time, by William Henry Fox Talbot (1800–77), '. . . how charming it would be if it were possible to cause these natural images to imprint themselves durably, and remain fixed upon the paper.' The answer lay in the darkening of silver salts on exposure to light.

In 1727 Dr. Johann Heinrich Schulze (1687–1744), a German physician, professor of anatomy and student of ancient medicine, discovered that light, not heat, darkened a solution of chalk and silver nitrate. By means of stencils laid over bottles of the solution he achieved exact representations of alphabet letters. Next, Carl Wilhelm Scheele (1742–86), a Swedish apothecary, furthered the investigations into light and its effect on silver salts, publishing his findings in 1777; while the Swiss Jean Senebier (1742–1809) found that certain resins hardened on exposure to light.

In England during the very last years of the eighteenth century Thomas Wedgwood (1771–1805), son of the potter, produced images of leaves, ferns and similar objects by laying them on white leather sensitized with silver nitrate. But he was unable to 'fix' the results and they could only be viewed by candlelight in subdued surroundings.

Eventually it was in France, in the 1820s, that Nicéphore Niépce (1765–1833) took and fixed the world's first successful photographs.

Frustratingly little is yet known of this momentous achievement. Joseph Nicéphore Niépce, a French army officer, aided at first by his brother Claude, a naval officer, began his experiments in about 1815/6. It seems that his initial aim was simply to produce 'copy photographs' on metal of old engravings for etching and then printing from in the conventional way. This he managed to do, and several heliographs (as his photographs were called) were successfully made for this purpose; basically by coating plates of metal (zinc, pewter or silver) with bitumen of Judea, which hardens on exposure to light, laying the original prints on top and exposing them to the sun. Following exposure the unhardened areas were removed by the careful application of a solvent (oil of lavender and petroleum) leaving the hardened bitumen to represent the lighter areas of the picture.

Niépce then managed to capture the image made by the camera obscura in a similar fashion. In 1826 he took and fixed the first photograph that is known to exist. It is the result of an 8-hour exposure; taken from an upstairs window at his home near Châlon-sur-Saône, in which he used a pewter plate coated with bitumen of Judea fixing the image by washing with a solvent as before. (This amazing photograph is now in the Gernsheim Collection at the University of Texas; and it is to Helmut Gernsheim who performed the act of rediscovery and research that the whole history of photography world is thankfully in debt.)

The Société Française de Photographie has in Paris a copy of a Niépce heliograph on glass, depicting a table covered with a cloth and laid for a fairly frugal meal. The original is long since lost or destroyed, but it has been claimed that this was taken in 1822. The claim may be justified for glass was indeed one of the base materials used by Niépce in his earliest experiments, nothing is completely certain and the date of 1829 suggested by Helmut Gernsheim may be more accurate.

During the next few years progress seems to have been fairly slow, and in 1829 Niépce, having found little enthusiasm for his achievements and probably feeling himself to be in a kind of cul-de-sac, joined forces with L. J. M. Daguerre (1787–1851), a painter and stage designer, who had been trying to fix the images made by the camera obscura since 1824/5. The partnership was a success and lasted right up to the death of Niépce in 1833.

Continuing the work himself Daguerre subsequently arrived at the first practicable photographic process, based on the darkening of silver salts rather than the hardening of bitumen. This he published in 1839.

Romantic tales spice Daguerre's actual discovery; however authentic they may be they can only add a very little colour to the overwhelming announcement of the process itself. 'Among all the mechanical poison that this terrible nineteenth century has poured upon man, it has given us at any rate one antidote—the Daguerreotype,' wrote Ruskin a few years later.

The Daguerreotype process employed copper plates, coated with silver and sensitized with iodine and/or bromine; after exposure the image was brought out, developed, with mercury vapour and finally fixed with hypo. There were no negatives and therefore one positive only was produced from each exposure.

Meanwhile in England, William Henry Fox Talbot, the rich gentleman scientist, had independently arrived at a negative and positive process on paper. Learning of Daguerre's achievement he hurried to announce this, his Photogenic Drawing process, and then, in 1841, patent the improved version—the Calotype or Talbotype. This employed ordinary writing paper washed with silver nitrate and potassium iodine; before use this was further treated with gallo nitrate of silver. Following exposure the latent negative image was developed with a final dose of gallo nitrate of silver and then

2

fixed with hypo. The positive print was made by superimposing the negative over similarly prepared paper and exposure to the light.

Whereas Talbot had patented his process, the French government bought the Daguerreotype process from Daguerre for the free benefit of the world—although Daguerre had in fact taken out a patent to cover England just a few days before the process was published in Paris. The French government, in addition to giving a pension and the Legion of Honour to Daguerre and a pension to Niépce's son, Isidore, also made a financial deal with another Frenchman, Hippolyte Bayard (1801–87), who was just on the brink of perfecting his own negative and positive process akin to that of Talbot.

At all events, patents or not, now in the early 1840s two viable photographic processes were available. The way, if not entirely clear, was at least clearly indicated.

Chronology

1558   Detailed description of the camera obscura, by Giovanni Battista della Porta.

1727   Experiments with silver salts and their reaction to light, by Dr. Johann Heinrich Schulze.

c. 1800   Images of leaves, ferns etc. obtained by superimposition on leather sensitized with silver nitrate, by Thomas Wedgwood.

1820s   First successful photographs, by Nicéphore Niépce.

1834   First successful negatives, by William Henry Fox Talbot.

1838   Invention of the Stereoscope, by Sir Charles Wheatstone.

1839   19 August. The Daguerreotype process given 'free to the world'—although a patent had been taken out to cover England five days earlier.

1840   March. The first photographic studio opened, in New York, by Alexander Wolcott and John Johnson.

1841   8 February. Introduction, and patenting in England, of the Calotype or Talbo-type process, by William Henry Fox Talbot.

1842   Introduction of the Cyanotype or Blueprint process, by Sir John Herschel.

1847   Calotype Club formed.

1848   Introduction of the Albumen on Glass process, by Abel Niépce de Saint Victor.

1850   Introduction of Albumen Paper for printing, by L. D. Blanquart-Evrard.

1851   Introduction of the Wet Plate or Wet Collodion process, by Frederick Scott Archer.
Introduction of the Waxed Paper process, by Gustave Le Gray.
Société Héliographique founded.

1851/2   Introduction of the Ambrotype process, by Frederick Scott Archer and P. W. Fry.

1852/3   Introduction of the Ferrotype or Tintype process, by A. A. Martin.

1853   Photographic Society of London founded.

1854   Société Française de Photographie founded.
American Union thermoplastic patented, by Samuel Peck.

1855   Introduction of the Collotype and Carbon Print processes, by Alphonse Louis Poitevin.

1856   Introduction of the Oxymel process, by John Dillwyn Llewelyn.

1858   First photographs taken from the air, from a balloon, by Nadar.

1861   Introduction of the Tannin process, by Charles Russell.
Demonstration of the first colour representations, by Sir James Clerk Maxwell.

4

1864   Perfection of the Carbon Print process, by Sir Joseph Wilson Swan.

1864/5   Introduction of the Woodburytype process, by Walter Bentley Woodbury.

1869   Publication of the Subtractive system of 3-colour photography, by Louis Ducos du Hauron.

· 1871   Experiments with the Dry Plate or Gelatin Emulsion process, by Dr. Richard Leach Maddox.

· 1872   First photographic investigations of animal movement, by Eadweard Muybridge.

1873   Platinotype process patented, by William Willis.

1879   Introduction of Photogravure, by Karl Klic.

1891   Development of the Interference system of colour photography, by Gabriel Lippmann.
Introduction of the Photochromoscope camera for colour, by Frederic Eugene Ives.

1892   Linked Ring Brotherhood formed.

1894   Introduction of the Gum Print or Gum Bichromate process.

1895   Introduction of the Rotogravure, by Karl Klic.

1899   Introduction of the Ozotype process, by Thomas Manly.

1902   Photo-Secession founded.

1904   Introduction of the Oil Print process, by G. E. H. Rawlins.
First successful colour screen process patented, by A. and L. Lumière. Introduced commercially as the Autochrome three years later.
International Society of Pictorial Photographers founded.

1905   Introduction of the Ozobrome process, by Thomas Manly.

1907   Introduction of the Bromoil process, by E. J. Wall and C. Welborne Piper.

Photographers and Photographic Inventors

ABDULLAH FRÈRES

Turkish(?) portrait photographers.

Studio in Constantinople during the second half of the nineteenth century.

Illustration—87.

ADAM-SALOMON, Antoine Samuel (1811–81)

French sculptor and portrait photographer.

Active in photography from *circa* 1855, producing portraits (frequently with considerable retouching) in a bold and mildly dramatic style.

Failing eyesight in the mid 1870s hastened his retirement.

Illustration—156.

ADAMSON, Robert (1821–48)
(HILL and ADAMSON)

Scottish calotype photographer.

The technical partner of David Octavius Hill (q.v.).

Robert Adamson learnt the calotype process early in 1843 as his health was insufficiently robust for his chosen career in engineering. The partnership with Hill began later the same year and continued until 1847, when Adamson was forced to give it up.

He died the following year aged only 27.

Between them Hill and Adamson made about 2,000 calotypes, portraits and group photographs of life in the large cities and small fishing villages of Scotland; achieving some of the most artistically satisfactory results of any very early photography.

Illustrations—19, 20 and 21.

ALBERT, Joseph (1825–86)

German portrait photographer.

Active during the second half of the nineteenth century particularly with carte-devisite photography of German high society.

Improved the Collotype process, in black and white in 1873 and then in colour in 1876.

ALINARI, Leopoldo (died 1865) and Giuseppe (1836–90*)

Italian topographical and portrait photographers.

Active during the 1850s and 60s, with views of Italian towns and carte-de-visite photography.

(* 1900 is also recorded as the date of Giuseppe's death.)

AMERICAN STEREOSCOPE COMPANY

American photographic manufacturers and publishers.

Active in New York from *circa* 1900, publishing series of stereoscope slides.

ANDERSON, James (1813–77). Pseudonym of Isaac ATKINSON

6

English watercolour artist, topographical and copy photographer.

Active in photography in Rome from *circa* 1850, mainly with the Roman antiquities, architecture and sculpture.

ANGERER, Ludwig (1827–79) and Victor (1839–94)

Austrian portrait photographers.

Active in Vienna during the second half of the nineteenth century, particularly with carte-de-visite photography.

ANNAN, James Craig (1864–1946)

Scottish portrait and artist photographer.

The son of Thomas Annan.

Although continuing his father's studio in Sauchiehall Street, Glasgow, James Craig Annan concentrated mostly on creative, purist photography; frequently employing the photogravure process which he had introduced to Scotland.

Member of the Linked Ring Brotherhood.

First president of the International Society of Pictorial Photographers, 1904.

Published in 1896 *Venice & Lombardy*, a folio of 11 photogravures, limited to 75 copies.

Illustrations—225 and 242.

ANNAN, Thomas (1829–87)

Scottish portrait and topographical photographer.

Studio in Sauchiehall Street, Glasgow.

Between 1868 and 1877 he made a photographic record of the Glasgow slums, for the Glasgow City Improvement Trust.

Thomas Annan also opened a carbon printing factory outside Glasgow where reproductions of Hill and Adamson calotypes were printed.

Illustration—65.

ANSCHÜTZ, Ottomar (1846–1907)

German animal and bird motion photographer.

Active from the early 1880s.

Invented in 1890 the Electrotachyscope, a rotating drum like apparatus in which very slightly different photographs of the same animal or bird were lit up and viewed in rapid succession to give the effect of motion.

ANTHONY, Edward (1818–88)

American daguerreotype, topographical and portrait photographer.

In 1841 Edward Anthony made a photographic survey of the American/Canadian border—a matter of dispute at the time.

In 1842, with J. M. Edwards, he opened a portrait studio in Washington, and then, a year later, he made a complete daguerreotype portrait library of the members of Congress.

Founded in 1852 E. & H. T. Anthony & Co., photographic publishers, manufacturers 'of the best photographic albums' and carte-de-visite photographers.

Illustration—68.

ARCHER, Frederick Scott (1813–57)

English sculptor, calotype and portrait photographer and photographic inventor.

Frederick Scott Archer learnt the calotype process as an aid to his sculpture, but it is for his invention of the Wet Plate or Wet Collodion process in 1851 that his name is never to be forgotten.

A year later, with P. W. Fry, he developed the Ambrotype process.

Declining to patent his inventions, and drawing no reward from their exploitation, he died a poor man.

ATGET, Jean Eugène Auguste (1856–1927)

French sailor, comedy actor, genre and documentary photographer.

From 1898 made an extensive photographic record of Paris, the people and the buildings, exteriors and interiors, shop fronts, shop signs, rich interiors and poor interiors, compiled in albums with titles as—*Enseignes et Vielles Boutiques du Vieux Paris* (early 1900s) and *Interieurs Parisiens, Artistiques, Pittoresques & Bourgeois* (early 1910).

Atget was unsponsored and managed to sell only a comparatively small proportion of his great work. He died a poor man.

Illustrations—207, 208, 209, 210, 211 and 212.

BABBITT, Platt D.

American daguerreotype photographer.

In 1853 granted the monopoly to photograph on the American side of Niagra Falls, enabling him to satisfy the demands of tourists for photographs of themselves *in situ*, the torrent forming a suitably grand background.

Illustration—10.

BALDRY, Alfred Lys (born 1858)

English painter and artist photographer.

With W. J. Day, produced a series of photographs of nude and draped figure subjects with titles as 'On the Brink', 'The Wishing Well' and 'Sea Frolic'.

Illustration—223.

BALDUS, Edouard Denis (1820–82)

Prussian born (French naturalized) painter, landscape and topographical photographer.

Active from the early 1850s producing large format, fine and sharp photographs of architecture (notably the Louvre in 1854–5) and sculpture.

In June 1865 made photographic record of the floods in southern France.

Founder member of the Société Héliographique, 1851.

Prints may be signed in facsimile on the mount.

Illustration—99.

BARRAUD, William

English portrait photographer.

Studios in London and Liverpool during the second half of the nineteenth century.

Illustrated *Men & Women of the Day*, 2 volumes, 1888 and 1889.

'Mr. Barraud's studios are approached by a lift constructed on the most approved patents which will be found a great advantage to sitters as no stairs have to be ascended.' (Cabinet portrait reverse.)

BASSANO, Alexander

English portrait photographer.

Studios in London from the third quarter of the nineteenth century.

His firm remains in active business having recently acquired Elliott & Fry.

BAYARD, Hippolyte (1801–87)

French civil servant, calotype and daguerreotype photographer and photographic inventor.

Experimented with photography from 1837.

Hippolyte Bayard came close to perfecting his own paper negative and positive process, but he was bought out by the French government to avoid prejudicing their announcement of the daguerrotype process in August 1839. Believing Daguerre's method of direct positives to be superior to his own process he ceased his experiments.

Later he turned to the calotype (which was in fact very similar to the process he had so nearly perfected) as well as the daguerreotype for his own photography.

Founder member of the Société Héliographique, 1851, and the Société Française de Photographie, 1854.

Illustrations—17 and 18.

BEARD, Richard (1801/2–85)

English coal merchant, patent speculator and daguerreotype photographer.

The first to open a photographic studio in England—at the Royal Polytechnic Institution, 309 Regent Street, London—in March 1841. Opened further studios in London, at 34 Parliament Square and 85 King William Street, and several in the provinces, Manchester and Liverpool (in partnership with James F. Foard).

Patented in 1842 the colouring of daguerreotypes.

Richard Beard is said to have amassed a fortune in quick time, but then lost it at a similar speed in law suits defending patent rights. Bankrupt in 1850.

Beard's daguerreotype portraits, well finished in cases marked with his name, remain in fairly large numbers—although it is possible that he never actually took any of the photographs himself and that they were all taken by his assistants.

Illustration—8.

BEATO, Felice A.

English(?) topographical, landscape and war photographer.

In partnership with James Robertson, Felice Beato travelled and photographed in the Middle and Near East, recording the Indian Mutiny, 1857–8. Later, alone, in the Far East he recorded the Chinese Opium War of 1860.

Published in 1868 *Views in Japan*.

Prints may be signed in the plate.

Illustration—40.

BEAU, Adolphe

French(?) portrait photographer.

Active in London during the second half of the nineteenth century, in association with Camille Silvy and later, with a Regent Street studio, in partnership with –. Heath.

Illustration—85.

BEDFORD, Francis (1816–94)

English topographical and landscape photographer.

Very active during the second half of the nineteenth century, Francis Bedford produced photographs of a consistently high standard—for issue as single prints, in sets and in carte-de-visite format. He made several series of stereoscope slides with titles as *Devonshire Illustrated*, *Herefordshire Illustrated* and *North Wales Illustrated*.

In 1862 travelled with the Prince of Wales in the Near East; later publishing 175 views.

Contributed to *The Sunbeam*, 1859, and the 1862 edition of William and Mary Howitt's *Ruined Abbeys and Castles of Great Britain and Ireland*, books illustrated by photographs.

Illustration—128.

BEKEN, Frank William (1880–1970)
(**BEKEN** of **COWES**)

English chemist and marine photographer.

Based at Cowes, Isle of Wight, from the closing years of the nineteenth century.

Prolific and pre-eminent in marine photography, private yachts and sailing boats especially.

His firm remains in active business.

Illustration—190.

BERTSCH, Adolphe (died 1870/1)

French scientist, photographer and photographic inventor.

During the 1850s made photomicrographs of insects, fleas, caterpillars and lice.

Invented in 1860 a special miniature automatic camera.

BINGHAM, Robert J. (died 1870)

English chemist, daguerreotype, copy and topographical photographer.

One time assistant to the chemist and scientist Professor Michael Faraday.

Active in photography from the early

1840s. In Paris from the early 1850s, notably with –. Thompson at the Exhibition of 1855.

During the late 1850s Robert Bingham made numerous copy photographs of paintings by Paul Delaroche.

BIOW, Hermann (1810–50)

German daguerreotype photographer.

Studio at Altona, Hamburg, from September 1841.

From 1842 in partnership with C. F. Stelzner, photographing in May the same year the ruins left by a fire in Hamburg—the earliest news photographs.

BISSON, Louis (born 1814) and Auguste (born 1826)
(BISSON FRÈRES)

French daguerreotype, portrait, topographical and copy photographers.

The proprietors of a portrait studio in Paris at an early date, but best known for Alpine photography during the early 1860s, including (with extreme ceremony) a photograph from the summit of Mont Blanc.

Circa 1853/5 they made numerous copy photographs of Rembrandt's paintings.

Founder members of the Société Française de Photographie, 1854.

Illustration—153.

BLANQUART-EVRARD, Louis Désiré (1802–72)

French topographical photographer and photo-chemical manufacturer.

Introduced in May 1850 Albumen Print Paper.

Opened in 1851 a photographic printing works at Lille.

BOAK, M.
(BOAK and SONS)

English portrait, landscape and topographical photographer/s.

Active during the second half of the nineteenth century, with studios in Bridlington, Driffield and Malton, Yorkshire, for carte-de-visite and cabinet portrait photography.

Produced a series of topographical photographs of northern England, including church interiors—in particular the frescoes in Bridlington Priory Church.

BOISSONNAS, père
BOISSONNAS, Fred (1858–1947)

Swiss portrait, topographical and representational photographer/s.

Studio in Geneva from the middle of the nineteenth century.

Fred Boissonnas subsequently opened other studios in France. During the early twentieth century he photographed extensively in Greece and then, later, in Italy.

BOND, William Cranch (1789–1859)

American daguerreotype photographer.

Based at Cambridge, Massachusetts.

Exhibited a daguerreotype of the moon in the Great Exhibition of 1851.

BOOLE, A. and J.

English topographical photographers.

From 1875 made records of disappearing London buildings for The Society for Photographing Relics of Old London.

BOURNE, Samuel (1834–1912)
(BOURNE and SHEPHERD)

English traveller, topographical, genre and portrait photographer.

During the 1860s and 70s Samuel Bourne photographed extensively in distant areas of

India and the Himalayas. The results were published in books and albums.

Studio partnership with –. Shepherd in Simla, Calcutta and Bombay.

Prints may be signed in the plate, with his surname alone.

Illustrations—88 and 95.

BRADY, Mathew B. (1823–1896)

American daguerreotype, portrait and war photographer, and manufacturer of daguerreotype and ambrotype cases.

Having learnt the daguerreotype process from Samuel Morse, Mathew Brady opened studios in New York, 1844, and Washington, 1847, where the leading members of American life were systematically photographed.

Later Brady became the prime mover in the organization of photographers (which included Alexander Gardner and Timothy H. O'Sullivan) self commissioned to make a complete photographic record of the American Civil War, 1861–5. The results were subsequently published by Alexander Gardner in *Gardner's Photographic Sketch Book of the War*, 1866.

Published in 1850 *Gallery of Illustrious Americans*, illustrated by lithographs from his daguerreotypes.

BRAUN, Adolphe (1811–77)

French topographical, portrait, Alpine and copy photographer.

Active during the third quarter of the nineteenth century with views as stereoscope slides, ordinary prints and large panoramas made up from more than one negative.

During the late 1860s Braun made photographic copies of old master paintings in different European collections.

Published in 1859 *L'Alsace Photographié*, two very large volumes containing 120 topographical photographs.

Illustrations—53 and 54.

BUCQUET, Maurice (died 1921)

French artist, landscape and genre photographer.

Active during the close of the nineteenth century.

CALDESI and MONTECCHI
(L. CALDESI and COMPANY)
(CALDESI, BLANFORD and COMPANY)

Apparently the same basic firm but with different partnerships.

Portrait photographers—both Caldesi and Montecchi were Italian born.

Studios in London during the second half of the nineteenth century, particularly for carte-de-visite photography.

CAMERON, Henry Herschel Hay

English tea planter, actor and portrait photographer.

The son of Julia Margaret Cameron.

Portrait studio in Mortimer Street, London, from *circa* 1885 to 1900.

Illustration—110.

CAMERON, Julia Margaret (1815–79)

English portrait and artist photographer.

Active in photography from 1863 to 1875.

'It may amuse you, Mother, to try to photograph your friends during your solitude in Freshwater.' With these words Julia Margaret Cameron, aged 48, was given a complete photographic outfit by her daughter. Few presents can have led to such amazing results. During the following 12 years, in the converted hen house of her home on the Isle of Wight, Mrs. Cameron mastered the technique to take some of the most marvellous photographs of any period. Portraits and beautiful subject pictures.

Portraits; with supreme exploitation of the close-up and soft focus, of 'famous men and fair women' (her own words), of Thomas

Carlyle, Charles Darwin, Sir John Herschel, Alfred Lord Tennyson, W. M. Rossetti, Anthony Trollope, G. F. Watts, Mrs. Herbert Duckworth and Ellen Terry.

Subject photographs; some as illustrations to Tennyson's poetry and others of a near religious nature with strong pre-Raphaelite influence and titles as 'The Kiss of Peace', 'Yes or No' and 'Red and White Roses'.

In 1875 Mrs. Cameron and her husband left England for Ceylon. Very few photographs were taken again and there, on 26 January 1879, she died.

Prints, large format, are often fully inscribed, signed and dated on their card mounts, besides bearing the stamp of P. & D. Colnaghi, the London print dealers.

By all accounts an exceptionally kind person—though a determined and demanding worker—in clothes stained and smeared with all manner of photographic chemical, Mrs. Cameron extracted the very most the medium had to offer. Many of her photographs have technical faults and flaws, but through these there shines all her strength of character and sensitive art.

A wonderful woman, a great artist in photography.

Illustrations—102, 103, 104, 105, 106, 107, 108 and 109.

CARJAT, Etienne. (1828–1906)

French caricaturist, journalist and portrait photographer.

Studio in Paris from the mid 1850s for strong, straight portraits of famous people, writers and artists.

Illustrations—79 and 155.

CARROLL, Lewis (1832–98). Pseudonym of the Reverend Charles Lutwidge DODGSON

English university don, clergyman, writer, portrait and child photographer.

Engaged in photography between 1856 and 1880.

Ever famous as the author of *Alice in Wonderland* and *Alice Through the Looking Glass*, Lewis Carroll became an equally successful photographer of children, small girls, dressed and undressed, and a very few small boys, with super sensitive faces in gentle and, again, sensitive poses.

Portraits were achieved with similar skill. The clergy, leading writers and leading painters were his subjects—Tennyson, Holman Hunt, Millais, Ellen Terry and Christina Rossetti.

Related poems and articles came as well —*Photography Extraordinary* (1855), *Hiawatha's Photographing* (1857) and *A Photographer's Day Out* (1860).

A great writer, a master photographer.

Illustrations—124, 125, 126 and 127.

CATHERWOOD, Frederick

English architect, daguerreotype and topographical photographer.

With John Lloyd Stephens, in 1841, made daguerreotype record of the 'lost cities' of Yucatan.

CHARNAY, Désiré (1828–1915)

French school teacher and topographical photographer.

During the late 1850s photographed the ancient Maya ruins, temples and sculpture, in Mexico, publishing the results in *Cités et Ruines Americaines* and *Fotografico Mexicano*— albums of large format photographs.

Illustration—52.

CIVIALE, Aimé (1821–93)

French army officer and topographical photographer.

Specialist in mountain photography, particularly the Alps during the 1860s and the Pyrenees during the 1880s.

Photographs may be signed in the plate.

CLAUDET, Antoine François Jean (1798–1867)

French glass merchant, daguerreotype and portrait photographer.

Antoine Claudet settled in England, *circa* 1829, and opened a studio in London, the Adelaide Gallery, in 1841—the second photographic studio ever in England.

Agent for the importing of French daguerreotypes and daguerreotype materials, he also made several scientific improvements to the process.

In 1851 Claudet opened the 'Temple of Photography', at 107 Regent Street, London, and then, later, turned his attention to carte-de-visite photography.

Often hailed as one of the best, the most artistic of all daguerreotype portrait photographers.

CLIFFORD, Charles (died 1863)

English landscape, topographical and portrait photographer.

Active in Madrid, Spain, from *circa* 1852.

Employed the calotype, waxed paper and wet plate processes for handsome topographical photographs.

Published in 1856 *Vistas del Capricho*, an album of 50 views of a palace near Guadalajara, and in 1858 *Voyages en Espagne*.

Prints are frequently signed in the plate.

Illustration—42.

COBURN, Alvin Langdon (1882–1966)

American portrait, landscape and artist photographer.

Active in New York from the very early 1900s, with a studio for exhibiting photographs in 1902 and his first one man exhibition in 1903.

A year or so later, in England, Alvin Langdon Coburn produced a series of portraits of famous men in a one man exhibition in 1906, and a collection of impressionistic landscape photographs of London—some for publication in 1909 as photogravures in a book entitled *London*, with an introduction by Hilaire Belloc.

At this time Coburn used a specially made soft focus lens and a gum platinum printing process to give an improved, more intensely shaded platinotype.

Later he became very experimental with such enterprises as 'New York from its Pinnacles', 1913, and the first ever purely abstract photographs, Vortographs, 1917.

Illustrated G. K. Chesterton's *London*, 1914.

Published in 1966 *Alvin Langdon Coburn, Photographer*, edited by Helmut and Alison Gernsheim.

Illustrations—244 and 245.

COLLEN, Henry (1800–75)

English miniature painter and calotype photographer.

The first licensee of the calotype process.

Opened a calotype studio in London in August 1841, although many of his portraits were used simply as bases for drawing over.

Collen probably assisted William Henry Fox Talbot with the artistic composition of Talbot's own calotype photographs.

COLLIE, W.

English calotype photographer.

Active in Jersey, the Channel Islands, during the 1840s.

CONSTABLE, William

English daguerreotype photographer.

Studio in Brighton, Sussex, from *circa* 1841.

Examples of William Constable's portrait daguerreotypes remain in fairly large numbers.

CORBETT, J.

New Zealand portrait photographer.

Studio in Auckland, New Zealand, during the second half of the nineteenth century.

Produced a fine series of carte-de-visite photographs of Maori people.

Illustrations—89 and 90.

CUNDALL, Joseph (1818–95)

English portrait, topographical and landscape photographer.

Contributed to *The Sunbeam*, 1859, a book of photographs edited by P. H. Delamotte.

Joseph Cundall's studio partnerships are confusing. At different dates it seems he was with Robert Howlett, –. Downes and –. Fleming.

CURTIS, Edward S. (1868–1952)

American genre photographer.

Recorded American Indians, their lives and looks.

Published, from *circa* 1890 to 1920, *North American Indians*, 20 volumes of photogravures in a limited edition of 500.

DAGRON, Prudent René Patrice (1819–1900)

French portrait and topographical photographer.

Studio in Rue Nve. des Petits Champs, Paris.

Produced some of the earliest microphotographs—of Paris, for inclusion in souvenirs, and also of messages for a pigeon post during the siege of Paris in 1870.

DAGUERRE, Louis Jacques Mandé (1787–1851)

French painter, stage designer and inventor of photography.

During the 1820s Daguerre was the inventor/manager of the Diorama, a kind of mobile, part transparent, architectural and landscape panorama displayed in auditoriums in Paris and London.

About 1824/5 he began his attempts to fix the image made by the camera obscura.

In 1829 he entered into partnership with Nicéphore Niépce to further their photographic explorations and experiments. Following Niépce's death in 1833, Daguerre continued the work eventually discovering the first ever practicable photographic process, a direct positive on a silvered copper plate— the Daguerreotype. The process was announced and given 'free to the world' by the French government on 19 August 1839 (although a patent had been taken out in England 5 days before).

Awarded a pension and the Legion of Honour by the French government in exchange for the process.

Published in 1839 *History and Practice of Photogenic Drawing on the True Principles of the Daguerreotype.*

At the present time less than 20 daguerreotypes taken by Daguerre are known to exist.

Illustration—3.

DANCER, John Benjamin (1812–77)

English daguerreotype photographer and photographic manufacturer.

Active in Liverpool, and then Manchester, from the early 1840s, notably in microphotography and such curiosities as the Ten Commandments on a photograph the size of a pin head.

Manufactured the first binocular stereoscope camera in 1853, and the improved version 3 years later.

DAVID, J.

French(?) portrait photographer.

Based in Paris during the last quarter of the nineteenth century.

DAVISON, George (1856–1930)

British anarchist, naturalistic and impressionistic artist photographer.

A follower of Peter Henry Emerson and naturalistic photography.

In 1890 George Davison took the first impressionistic photograph—'The Onion Field'.

Founder member of the Linked Ring Brotherhood, 1892.

For 14 years managing director of Kodak Ltd.; a position which he had to resign in 1912 for his political proclivities.

Illustration—221.

DAY, Frederick Holland (1864–1933)

American representational, nude, portrait and artistic photographer.

'... the most daring apostle of the camera ... talked about in two continents' (*The Boston Herald* of 17 January 1899).

During the late 1890s Frederick Holland Day made a series of photographs of set piece religious subjects, including The Crucifixion, in 1898, staged on a hill 20 miles from Boston.

Later, in the early 1900s, he produced some very fine and gentle photographs of the male nude.

Member of the Linked Ring Brotherhood and Photo-Secession.

The platinotype was his preferred process, and prints may be signed with his initials— and sometimes the date as well—in red.

Illustrations—248, 249 and 250.

DAY, W. J.

English portrait and artist photographer.

Active in Bournemouth during the end of the nineteenth century and early twentieth century.

With A. L. Baldry, produced a series of photographs of nude and draped figure subjects with titles as 'On the Brink', 'The Wishing Well' and 'Sea Frolic'.

Circa 1905 produced a further series of his own—'Studies on Land and Sea', a collection of 'pure' sea and cloud photographs.

Illustration—223.

DELAMOTTE, Philip Henry (1820–89)

English graphic artist, calotype, topographical and documentary photographer.

Edited in 1859 *The Sunbeam*, a book illustrated with 'photographs from nature' by photographers as Francis Bedford, Joseph Cundall, George Washington Wilson and, also, he himself.

Published in 1855 *Photographic Views of the Progress of the Crystal Palace, Sydenham, Taken During the Process of Works, by Desire of the Directors*, 2 volumes of photographs based on his work of documentation between 1851 and 1854.

Illustration—116.

DEMACHY, Robert (died 1937)

French aristocrat, banker, painter and impressionistic photographer.

Active from *circa* 1896, especially employing the gum print process for photographs made to closely resemble hand executed drawings.

Member of the Linked Ring Brotherhood.

Founder of the Photo-Club de Paris.

Prints are generally signed with his initials, in red, on the surface.

Illustrations—228 and 230.

DEMENY, Georges (1850–1917)

French scientist and motion photographer.

From 1882 to 1894 assistant to Etienne Marey.

Published, with Etienne Marey, in 1893 in several parts *Etude de Physiologie Artistique, Des Mouvements de L'homme*, and on his own in 1909 *Les Origines du Cinématographie*.

Illustration—179.

DEVENS, Mary

English artist, figure and landscape photographer.

Active *circa* 1900.

Prints may be signed with her initials.

DIAMOND, Hugh W. (1809–86)

English doctor, calotype photographer and photographer of mental patients and topography.

Active in photography from the early 1840s.

Between 1848 and 1858, as superintendent of the female patients at Surrey County Asylum, Dr. Diamond made several series of very rare, beautiful and sympathetic, portraits of the mentally ill, as records and as aids for treating the sitters themselves.

Illustrations—23, 24, 25 and 26.

DISDÉRI, André Adolphe Eugène (1819–c. 1890)

French portrait photographer.

The great exponent and probable inventor of Carte-de-Visite photography.

Portrait studios from the early 1850s in Paris (Boulevard des Italiens), London (Brook Street, Hanover Square), Madrid and Toulon.

Greatly helped by the early patronage of Napoleon III, Disdéri amassed a fortune satisfying the demands for carte-de-visite photographs.

Following the decline in interest in the carte-de-visite he quickly ran through his money, ending his days as a beach photographer and in near poverty.

Disdéri's carte-de-visite photographs still exist in vast numbers, standing out in any portrait album on immediately obvious merit.

Illustrations—55, 59 and 60.

DIXON, Henry

English miniature painter, portrait and topographical photographer.

Studio at 112 Albany Street, Regent's Park, London.

From 1875 made records of disappearing London buildings for The Society for Photographing Relics of Old London—starting with the Oxford Arms, Warwick Lane, a well known inn pending demolition.

Illustration—144.

DOWNEY, W. and D.

English portrait photographers.

Studios in Ebury Street, London, and in Newcastle-on-Tyne, during the second half of the nineteenth century, with carte-de-visite and cabinet portrait photography of a consistently high standard.

Illustrated *The Cabinet Portrait Gallery*, 1890.

Illustrations—161 and 162.

DRAPER, John William (1811–82)

American doctor, scientist and early daguerreotype photographer.

Opened a portrait studio at New York University with Samuel Morse in the spring of 1840.

DU CAMP, Maxime (1822–94)

French calotype and topographical photographer.

In 1849 travelled in the Near East, particularly Egypt, with the writer Gustave Flaubert, photographing the pyramids and sphynx.

Published in 1851 *Egypte*, *Nubie*, *Palestine et Syrie*, illustrated by more than 100 photographs.

Illustration—31.

DUCHENNE, Guillaume Benjamin Amant (1806–75)

French doctor and physiognomical photographer.

Inventor of Electro Therapy.

Contributed to Charles Darwin's *The Expressions of the Emotions in Man and Animals*, 1872.

Published in 1862 *Album de Photographies Pathologiques*.

DUCOS du HAURON, Louis (1837–1920)

French pioneer of colour photography.

In 1877 Louis Ducos du Hauron took the

earliest colour photograph known to exist—a view of Angoulême.

Published in 1869 *Les Couleurs en Photographie, Solution du Problème*, a treatise based on the Subtractive System.

DUFFIN, S.

Canadian(?) portrait and genre photographer.

Active from Winnipeg during the second half of the nineteenth century, particularly with genre photographs of the North American Indians.

DÜHRKOOP, Rudolph (1848–1918)

German portrait and artist photographer.

Active *circa* 1900, employing controlled print processes.

DURAND, J. E.

French topographical photographer.

Active in Paris during the end of the nineteenth century.

EAKINS, Thomas (1844–1916)

American painter, sculptor and motion photographer.

Active in the photographic investigation of animal and human movement in Philadelphia, *circa* 1884/5, using a single camera with revolving shutters.

EASTMAN, George (1854–1932)

American photographic inventor and founder of Kodak.

Having patented a machine for coating dry plates in 1879, Eastman produced, in 1884/5, the first manageable roll film, and then, in 1888, the Kodak 'box' camera.

By 1900 Kodak had become the largest photographic manufacturers in the world.

EASTMEAD, J. J.

English photographer.

Active from Rochester, Kent, during the during the second half of the nineteenth century.

In June 1870 photographed the auction sale of furniture that had belonged to Charles Dickens.

ELLIOTT, J.

English genre and humour photographer.

Active during the third quarter of the nineteenth century, particularly with stereoscope slides of children, middle class domestic scenes and activities, in studios as set groups. Many were hand coloured, some were sold as transparencies and some were published by the London Stereoscopic & Photographic Company.

ELLIOTT and FRY

English portrait photographers.

Studio in Baker Street, London, from the second half of the nineteenth century for carte-de-visite and cabinet portrait photography especially and, later, 'At Home' photography.

Great quantities of their photographs exist today—mostly in portrait albums.

The firm remains in active business, but now as a part of Bassano.

Illustrations—63 and 163.

ELLIS, Alexander John (1814–90)

English doctor, mathematician, antiquarian and daguerreotype photographer.

In 1840–1 Dr. Ellis took the earliest surviving photographs, daguerreotypes, of Italian architecture—inscribing, describing and fully dating several of the plates.

Illustrations—5 and 6.

EMERSON, Peter Henry (1856–1936)

English (American father, English mother) doctor, writer and naturalistic artist photographer.

The son of a doctor, and having himself qualified in 1885, Emerson immediately gave up medicine for writing and the photography of life in East Anglia, the Norfolk broads and marshes.

In reaction to the composed pictorialism of the second half of the nineteenth century he pursued a natural style of photography, involving simple and familiar scenes, manners and ways.

'After many practical experiments I found the closest truth to nature in photography (from the psychological point of view) was to be obtained by throwing the background of the picture out of focus to an extent which did not produce destruction of structure— that was my limit; the principal object of the picture being sharp or just out of sharp. This convention I termed the naturalistic method of focusing . . .' (*Naturalistic Photography*, 1889.)

Publications include—*Life and Landscape on the Norfolk Broads*, 1886, produced with the help of the painter T. F. Goodall and illustrated with 40 platinotypes.

Pictures from Life in Field and Fen, 1887, a folio of 20 photogravures, with an introduction dedicated to Nicophore Niépce [*sic*].

Naturalistic Photography, 1889.

The Death of Naturalistic Photography, 1890.

Wild Life on a Tidal Water, 1890, illustrated with photo-etchings by himself and T. F. Goodall.

Marsh Leaves, 1895, illustrated with 16 photo-etchings.

Highly sensitive and articulate Peter Henry Emerson led the school of naturalistic photography. He was the most influential figure in art photography during the close of the nineteenth century.

From about 1900 he disappeared more or less completely from the photographic world.

Illustrations—217, 218, 219 and 220.

ENGLAND, William (died 1896)

English topographical photographer.

Chief photographer to the London Stereoscopic & Photographic Company during the 1850s and until 1863.

Photographed Blondin crossing Niagara Falls on a tight-rope, 1859.

During the mid 1860s William England specialized in Swiss and Alpine photography, publishing views as stereoscope slides 'Under the Special Patronage of the Alpine Club'.

Invented in 1861 the focal plane shutter.

ERFURTH, Hugo (1874–1948)

German portrait and artist photographer.

Active at Dresden from the mid 1890s, particularly employing controlled print processes.

EVANS, Frederick Henry (1852–1943)

English bookseller and topographical photographer.

The artist of a very beautiful series of photographs of cathedrals, interiors and exteriors, started in 1896. Also a similarly successful portrait of Aubrey Beardsley.

Member of the Linked Ring Brotherhood.

A strong advocate of 'straight' representation, Frederick Evans invariably used the platinotype process for his paper prints and gave up photography after the first world war when platinum ceased to be readily available.

Prints are usually impressed with his initials.

Illustrations—232, 233 and 234.

FENTON, Roger (1819–69)

English lawyer, painter, landscape, topographical, still life and war photographer.

Born in Lancashire Roger Fenton came to be one of the great nineteenth century photographers. His beautiful calm landscapes and perfect still life photographs are among the very finest to be seen within the medium—in any period.

Travelled and photographed in Russia, 1851–2.

Primarily, though, his name is inextricably associated with the Crimean War, 1853–6. During 1855 he took nearly 400 photographs of the conflict; travelling, living and working in a specially built 'photographic van'.

Founder and first secretary of the Photographic Society of London, January 1853—now the Royal Photographic Society of Great Britain.

Contributed to the 1862 edition of William and Mary Howitt's *Ruined Abbeys and Castles of Great Britain and Ireland*.

Illustrations—37, 50 and 51.

FERRIER, J. A. and C. M. (1811–89)

French topographical photographers.

Active during the third quarter of the nineteenth century, particularly with European topography and Alpine subjects especially: many of the photographs, taken in partnership with Charles Soulier, were published as stereoscope slides on glass.

Recorded in 1859, also as stereoscope slides, the French troubles over Austria and Sardinia.

FORBES-WHITE, John (1831–1904)

Scottish doctor, calotype, landscape and topographical photographer.

Active from the early 1850s.

Prints may be signed in the plate with his initials and date.

FOUCAULT, Jean Bernard Léon (1819–68)

French physicist, scientist and daguerreotype photographer. In 1844–5 Jean Foucault took the first photographs of the sun.

Illustration—7.

FREDERICKS, Charles D.

American portrait photographer.

Studio in New York during the second half of the nineteenth century.

Illustration—67.

FRITH, Francis (1822–98)

English landscape and topographical photographer.

During the second half of the nineteenth century Francis Frith was probably the most prolific topographical photographer and publisher of topographical photographs there was. He travelled and worked extensively—in the British Isles, Europe and the East.

Founder of Francis Frith & Company, printers and publishers, of Reigate, Surrey. The firm remained in active business until very recently.

Illustrated Henry Longfellow's *Hyperion*, 1865.

Published in 1864 *The Gossiping Photographer at Hastings*.

Frith's high quality photographs, which were sold in albums, in folio form, in series of stereoscope slides and singly for collections, may be signed with his name in the plate, or marked 'F.F. & Co.', or finely embossed 'Frith's Series'. It seems likely that only those with his name in the plate are certainly by him and that the others are by assistants.

Illustrations—111, 112 and 113.

GALE, Joseph (died 1906)

English army colonel, genre, landscape and naturalistic photographer.

Active during the close of the nineteenth century.

Illustration—224.

GARDNER, Alexander (1821–82)

Scottish born portrait, survey and war photographer.

In America from 1856.

The manager of the Washington studio of Mathew B. Brady until 1863. His own studios, also in Washington, from 1863 to 1867, mainly for carte-de-visite photography.

During the American Civil War, 1861–5, Alexander Gardner became the most prominent member of the team of photographers organized by Mathew B. Brady to record the hostilities.

Published in 1866 *Gardner's Photographic Sketch Book of the War*, 2 volumes involving 100 photographs.

Illustrations—70, 71, 72 and 73.

GAUDIN, Marc Antoine Augustine (1804–80)

French scientist, daguerreotype and portrait photographer.

Active from *circa* 1840/1, particularly with 'instantaneous' daguerreotypes of Paris.

GELL, R. E. E.

South African photographer.

Active from Newcastle, Natal, notably with straight reportage photographs of the Boer War, 1899–1902.

Illustrations—203 and 204.

GENTHE, Arnold (1868–1942)

German born doctor, sociological, genre and portrait photographer.

Active from *circa* 1895 in San Francisco, recording in particular the people of Chinatown and the aftermath of the earthquake in 1906.

Later in New York with portraits of the famous and fashionable.

Published in 1937 *As I Remember*, his autobiography.

GIRAULT de PRANGEY, Joseph Philibert (1804–92/3)

French painter, daguerreotype and topographical photographer.

In Paris during 1841–2 and widely active in the Levant, Egypt and Asia Minor a year or two later.

Girault de Prangey produced comparatively large format (9 in. by 7 in.) daguerreotypes of architecture, sculpture and topography.

Daguerreotypes may be incised with his signature and the title.

Illustration—4.

GORDON, R.

English landscape photographer.

Active from Bembridge, Isle of Wight, during the middle of the nineteenth century.

GROOM and COMPANY

English marine photographers.

Based at Plymouth, Devon, during the third quarter of the nineteenth century.

Illustration—100.

GRUNDY, William Morris (1806–59)

English patent-leather manufacturer and genre photographer.

Birmingham born and based.

Engaged in photography during the last 5 years of his life, William Grundy achieved notable success with a series of stereoscope slides of simple genre subjects entitled 'Rural England'.

HAWARDEN, Viscountess Clementina (1822–65)

Scottish born portrait and artist photographer.

Lady Hawarden's slightly strange photographs of women, ladies and children, in groups, separately, by windows, by mirrors, sometimes even dressed as men, were much admired in the mid nineteenth century—particularly by Lewis Carroll.

Illustrations—120, 121, 122 and 123.

HEATH, Vernon (1819–95)

English calotype, landscape and portrait photographer.

Studio—'Royal Photographic Studio'—at 43 Piccadilly, London.

Published in 1891 *Recollections*, his autobiography.

HEDDERLY, James (*c.* 1815–85)

English sign writer and topographical photographer.

Active in photography from 1865, particularly with fine large format photographs of London, the river Thames and Chelsea especially.

Addresses at Duke Street, Chelsea, and 21 Riley Street, Chelsea.

Illustration—117.

HENDERSON, A. L. (died 1900)

English portrait photographer, photo-scientist and 'photographer in enamel'.

Active during the second half of the nineteenth century.

Studios in London and New Cross.

During the 1860s and 70s specialized in photo-ceramics—positive photographic prints on porcelain plaques.

Illustration—77.

HENNAH, T. H.
(HENNAH and KENT)

English portrait photographer/s.

Studio in Brighton, Sussex, during the second half of the nineteenth century.

'Landscape and Animal Photography by appointment'. (Carte-de-visite reverse.)

Illustration—84.

HENNEMAN, Nicolaas (born 1813)

Dutch born calotype and portrait photographer.

Assistant to William Henry Fox Talbot at Reading, Berkshire.

In 1847 opened a portrait studio in Regent Street, London, employing the calotype process. He later changed to the wet plate.

HERSCHEL, Sir John Frederick William (1792–1871)

English astronomer, scientist and photographic inventor.

Within one week of hearing rumours of Daguerre's discoveries, in January 1839, Sir John Herschel was taking his own photographs. They were on paper, sensitized with carbonate of silver and fixed—through his own earlier discovery—with sodium thiosulphate (hypo).

Conjured the terms 'photograph', 'negative', 'positive' and 'snapshot'.

Invented in June 1842 the Cyanotype or Blueprint process.

HESLER, Alexander (1823–95)

American daguerreotype, ambrotype, topographical and portrait photographer.

Studio in Chicago from *circa* 1852.

Founder of Hesler's Photographic and Fine Art Gallery, '... the most extensive establishment of the kind in the world ...' where 'Daguerreotypes and Ambrotypes of every style and size' could be taken or acquired.

A series of daguerreotypes of the Mississippi River, including the Minnehaha Falls, and a portrait of Abraham Lincoln, are among Hesler's most spectacular successes.

HILL, David Octavius (1802–70)
(HILL and ADAMSON)

Scottish painter and calotype photographer.

David Octavius Hill became interested in photography whilst planning a large commemorative painting of the Signing of the Act of Separation of the Free Church of Scotland, in May 1843. In August he was introduced to Robert Adamson (q.v.), who had just started calotype photography in Edinburgh, in the belief that calotype portraits would be a help in painting the 450 clergy and dignitaries involved. The belief was justified, and Hill and Adamson entered into a partnership which was to have the most successful consequences.

Between 1843 and 1847 they made around 2,000 calotype photographs (mostly 8 in. by 6 in. contact prints) of life at all levels in the large cities and small fishing villages of Scotland; achieving some of the finest results of any very early photography.

Hill's genial, charming and vital personality was no doubt a strong factor in the partnership with the ailing Adamson, who had to give up in 1847 and who died the following year aged only 27.

Secretary of the Royal Scottish Academy, Hill continued his other activities until 1860 when he tried, not very successfully, a return to photography with A. McGlashan.

Published in 1862 *Contributions Towards the Further Development of Fine Art in Photography*.

Since 1847 reproductions of Hill and Adamson calotypes, albeit from the original negatives, have been made on several occasions. The series of carbon prints produced by Thomas Annan at the end of the nineteenth century springs very readily to mind.

Illustrations—19, 20 and 21.

HILL, Levi L. (1816–65)

American Baptist minister, writer, chemist and daguerreotype photographer.

In 1850 claimed to have perfected a colour daguerreotype process. As far as is known no examples remain.

Published in 1856 a *Treatise on Heliochromy*, an account of the mystery.

HILLS and SAUNDERS

English portrait photographers.

Studios in London, Eton, Harrow, Oxford and Sandhurst, for carte-de-visite and cabinet portrait photography especially, during the second half of the nineteenth century.

Illustration—86.

HINE, Lewis Wickes (1874–1940)

American sociological photographer.

Between 1905 and 1910 Hine made studies of the oppressed in America, the iron and steel workers, the miners, child labour, poor European immigrants.

Published *circa* 1908 *The Pittsburgh Survey*, and in 1932 *Men at Work*—a record of the construction of the Empire State Building.

Illustration—206.

HINTON, Alfred Horsley (1863–1908)

English graphic artist, illustrator and artist photographer.

Active during the end of the nineteenth century and early twentieth century, employing the gum print and other controlled print processes for gentle art photographs.

Leading founding member of the Linked Ring Brotherhood, 1892.

Published in 1894 *A Handbook of Illustration*.

Illustration—227.

HOFMEISTER, Theodor (1868–1943) and Oskar (1869–1937)

German landscape, genre and artist photographers.

Active from the mid 1890s and into the early twentieth century, particularly with gum print photographs of fishing and working people and landscapes.

Illustration—236.

HOLLYER, Frederick H. (1837–1933)

English landscape and portrait photographer.

Active from *circa* 1870, producing straight landscapes and very fine potraits of many of the leading writers and artists of the day.

Employed the carbon print process and then, later, the platinotype.

Illustrations—145, 146, 147, 148 and 149.

HOOPER, W. W.

English captain in the Madras Light Cavalry, reporting and topographical photographer.

Active with topography in London, *circa* 1875/6.

Captain Hooper photographed the victims of the Madras famine of 1876–7.

HOPPÉ, Emil Otto (1878–1972)

German born portrait and genre photographer.

Originally a bank clerk, in 1907 Hoppé opened a studio in London—first in Baker Street and then, in elaborate and expansive style, in South Kensington, for the portrayal of many famous men, and some women.

He later travelled and photographed in Africa, the Far East and Australasia.

Published in 1912 *Studies from the Russian Ballet*, a folio of 15 photographs, and in 1945 *Hundred Thousand Exposures*, his autobiography; 18 other books besides.

Illustration—251.

HORNE, Fallon (died 1858)

English portrait and artist photographer.

An early employer of the ambrotype process.

HOWLETT, Robert (died 1858)

English portrait photographer.

Studio partnership with Joseph Cundall at the Photographic Institution, Bond Street, London, from 1855.

In 1856 Robert Howlett made extensive photographic studies as aids to the painter W. P. Frith for his picture 'Derby Day'.

In 1858 he recorded the launching of the *Great Eastern*, having already photographed the ship's designer, I. K. Brunel, standing, boldly, cigar drooping, before a wall of massive iron chains—one of the most successful portraits ever, in any medium.

Illustration—41.

HUFFMAN, Laton Alton

American genre and portrait photographer.

Circa 1878/9 made photographic exposé of the indiscriminate mass slaughter of buffalo in the American mid west.

Studio in Miles City, Montana, from 1880.

HUGHES, Alice

English portrait photographer.

The daughter of the painter Edward Hughes.

Studios in London, from *circa* 1886, and in Berlin, from 1913. She later returned to London.

Active until the early 1920s, particularly with the portrayal of women.

Published in 1923 *My Father and I*, her autobiography.

HUGHES, Cornelius Jabez (1819–84)

English portrait photographer.

Active in Glasgow from 1849 and then London from 1855 (some of the time apparently with –. Meek).

Later studio at Ryde, Isle of Wight, in partnership with Gustav(?) Mullins.

Illustration—189.

HUGO, Charles Victor (1826–71)

French photographer.

The son of Victor Hugo.

With the poet Auguste Vacquerie, young

Hugo produced a rare series of photographs taken in Jersey, between 1853 and 1855, during his father's exile on the island.

Illustrations—32, 33 and 34.

ISENRING, Johann Baptist (1796–1860)

Swiss painter, engraver and daguerreotype photographer.

Active from 1839, particularly with daguerreotypes of St. Gallen, Switzerland.

Studio in Munich from 1841.

IVES, Frederic Eugene (1856–1937)

American printer, photographer and pioneer of colour photography.

Produced in 1891 the Photochromoscope camera and Kromskop viewer.

JACKSON, William Henry (1843–1942)

American water colour artist, topographical and genre photographer.

Studio at Omaha, Nebraska, with his brother from 1867. Later at Denver, Colorado.

During the 1870s Jackson accompanied seven American government geological surveys, producing about 1,000 stereoscope slides and 1,000 prints of the middle and far west of America.

JACOLETTE, Martin

English portrait and topographical photographer.

Studios in London and Dover, Kent, during the latter part of the nineteenth century.

Prints may be embossed with his surname.

JANSSEN, Pierre Jules César (1824–1907)

French astronomer, topographical and celestial photographer.

In 1874 photographed the transit of Venus across the Sun, using a camera with a special revolving mechanism for making exposures in rapid succession.

JOHNSON, John

American daguerreotype photographer.

With his partner, Alexander Wolcott, the first in the world to open a photographic studio, a 'Daguerrian Parlor', in New York early in March 1840.

JOHNSTON, John Dudley (1868–1955)

English artist photographer.

Active from the close of the nineteenth century, particularly in Switzerland, with some impressionistic, controlled process photography.

JULLIEN, J.

Swiss(?) topographical photographer.

Active during the second half of the nineteenth century, particularly with mountain photography.

Illustration—154.

KÄSEBIER, Gertrude (1852–1934)

American portrait and artist photographer.

Active during the close of the nineteenth century and early years of the twentieth century, with figure composition photographs.

Illustration—243.

KEENE, R.

English landscape and topographical photographer.

Active during the middle of the nineteenth century.

Exhibited a series of photographs of 'Derbyshire scenery and antiquities' in the Exhibition of 1862.

KEIGHLEY, Alexander (1861–1947)

English wool manufacturer and artist photographer.

Born and died at Keighley, Yorkshire.

Active from the early 1880s (and well into the 1940s), producing large format photographs of romantic subjects, impressionistic landscapes and genre, taken mostly in Mediterranean countries; frequently signing his name on the finished print.

Founder member of the Linked Ring Brotherhood, 1892.

Illustration—226.

KEILEY, Joseph T. (1869–1914)

American artist photographer.

Active during the close of the nineteenth century, particularly employing a special slight variant on the platinotype process.

KEITH, George Skene

Scottish doctor and daguerreotype photographer.

The brother of Thomas Keith.

Active from *circa* 1844, particularly with daguerreotypes of the Near East.

KEITH, Thomas (1827–95)

Scottish doctor and part time topographical photographer.

The brother of George Keith.

Active during the 1850s, in and around Edinburgh, using the calotype and waxed paper processes.

KEY, Frederick C.

American engraver and diesinker.

Active in New York and Philadelphia during the 1850s and 1860s, with designs for American Union cases.

KILBURN, William Edward

English daguerreotype and portrait photographer.

Daguerreotype studios in London (at 222 and 234 Regent Street) from a very early date.

Registered in January 1853 his own stereoscope and daguerreotype case combination.

He later turned to carte-de-visite photography.

Illustration—9.

KING, H. (1830–95)

English portrait photographer.

Studio in Bath, Somerset, during the second half of the nineteenth century.

KLIC, Karl (1841/2–1926)

Czechoslovakian painter and photographic inventor.

Introduced in 1879 the Photogravure process and then, in 1895, perfected the technique into Rotogravure.

KRONE, Hermann (1827–1916)

German daguerreotype, topographical and landscape photographer.

Active from the mid 1840s.

Published fine, high quality stereoscope slides of landscape and topography.

KÜHN, Heinrich (1866–1944)

German born artist photographer.

Active in Austria from the 1890s, employing the gum print process in particular for portrait and landscape photographs.

Member of the Linked Ring Brotherhood.

Illustration—229.

KUHN, J.

French(?) topographical photographer.

Based in Paris, 220 rue de Rivoli, during the second half of the nineteenth century.

KURTZ, William (born 1834)

German born soldier and sailor and portrait photographer.

Studios in New York, on Broadway from 1865 and Madison Square from 1874, for carte-de-visite and cabinet portrait photography.

LAFAYETTE

French portrait photographer.

Studios in Paris (from *circa* 1865), Dublin (from *circa* 1880), Glasgow and Manchester, for very fine quality carte-de-visite and cabinet portrait photography especially.

Illustration—158.

LAMY, E.

French topographical photographer.

Published stereoscope slides of European views, in series, during the second half of the nineteenth century.

LANGENHEIM, Wilhelm (1807–74) and Friedrich (1809–79)

German born daguerreotype, calotype, portrait and landscape photographers and photographic inventors.

Active in America, Philadelphia, from the early 1840s, notably with the calotype process from 1848.

Introduced in 1849 photographic lantern slides, Hyalotypes, made by the albumen on glass process.

LANGLOIS, Jean Charles (1789–1870)

French army officer ('Le Colonel'), painter of battle scenes, topographical and war photographer.

Active in the Crimea from 1855, subsequently publishing *Souvenirs de la Guerre de Crimée*, an album of large format photographs of the war areas taken by himself and L. Méhévin.

Illustrations—38 and 39.

LAROCHE, Silvester (1809–86)

Canadian born portrait photographer.

Studio partnership in Birmingham, England, with Napoleon Sarony, from 1864 to 1866.

LARTIGUE, Jacques Henri (born 1894)

French 'naïf', genre and landscape photographer.

Given a camera when only 7 years old. Ever since Lartigue has produced gentle, sensitive photographs of ordinary people in ordinary surroundings—generally middle class rather than working class.

An early exponent of colour photography employing the autochrome process.

LE GRAY, Gustave (1820–62)

French painter, calotype, portrait, sea and landscape photographer.

Portrait studio in Paris from 1848.

Introduced in 1851 the Waxed Paper process.

During the 1850s Gustave Le Gray took very distinctive and beautiful seascape photographs (large format) involving strong and intense cloud effects.

Founder member of the Société Héliographique, 1851.

Published in 1850 *A Practical Treatise on Photography*.

Prints may be signed, on the surface, in red.

Illustrations—97, 98 and 101.

LENNIE

Scottish topographical photographer.

Active from Princes Street, Edinburgh, during the second half of the nineteenth century, producing views in carte-de-visite format and as stereoscope slides.

LEREBOURS, Noel Marie Paymal (1807–73)

French optical instrument and camera manufacturer, portrait and nude photographer.

Manufacturer of daguerreotype and wet plate cameras.

Founder member of the Société Héliographique, 1851.

Published in 1841/2 *Excursions Daguerriennes*, a book illustrated with engravings from daguerreotypes taken by itinerant artists.

LE SECQ, Henri (1818–82)

French painter, still life, genre, landscape, topographical and copy photographer.

Active during the 1850s, employing the calotype and waxed paper processes for bold, strong photographs.

Founder member of the Société Héliographique, 1851.

Published in 1852 *Amiens: Recueil de Photographies* and *Paris Photographique* (an album printed by Blanquart-Evrard).

Illustration—22.

LINDT, J. W.

Australian portrait and genre photographer.

Based at Melbourne.

Circa 1875, he produced a rare series of photographs of the New South Wales Aborigines, singly and in groups, in studios set with their shelters and artefacts. Also, probably later, some similar photographs of the indigeneous people of New Guinea.

LIPPMANN, Gabriel (1845–1921)

French physicist and pioneer of colour photography.

Developed in 1891 the Interference System of colour photography.

LLEWELYN, John Dillwyn

Welsh(?) calotype and landscape photographer and photographic inventor.

Introduced in 1856 the Oxymel process.

Contributed to *The Sunbeam*, 1859, a book of photographs edited by Philip Delamotte.

LÖCHERER, Alois (1815–62)

German chemist, calotype, portrait, nude and genre photographer.

Active in Munich from the late 1840s.

Recorded in 1850 the transportation of the statue 'Bavaria' from the foundry to Munich's Hall of Fame.

LOHMANN, Helen

American portrait photographer.

Active in New York during the early twentieth century.

THE LONDON STEREOSCOPIC and PHOTOGRAPHIC COMPANY

English portrait and landscape photographers, and photographic publishers.

Portrait studios in London, at 54 Cheapside and 108–110 Regent Street.

Publishers of stereoscope slides, carte-devisite and cabinet portrait photographs for mass sale, throughout the second half of the nineteenth century.

Illustrations—82 and 130.

LOWE, R.

English daguerreotype photographer.

Studio in Cheltenham, Gloucestershire, during the mid nineteenth century.

LOWRIE, J. F.

English portrait photographer.

Studio in Fleet Street, London, during the end of the nineteenth century, particularly for tintype photographs mounted in cards of carte-de-visite format.

Illustration—170.

LUBOSHEZ, Nahum Ellan (1869–1925)

Russian born portrait, genre and reportage photographer.

Active in Hamburg, Germany, during the 1890s and in Russia during the very early twentieth century.

LUMIÈRE, Auguste (1862–1954) and Louis (1864–1948)

French scientists, photographic manufacturers and pioneers of colour photography and cinematography.

Patented in 1904 the first successful colour screen process, which was introduced commercially as the Autochrome in 1907.

LYTE, Farnham Maxwell (1828–1906)

English calotype, topographical and landscape photographer.

Active during the middle of the nineteenth century, particularly with photographs of mountains in Europe.

Prints may be signed in full on the mounts.

MACAIRE, Hippolyte

French daguerreotype photographer.

Active *circa* 1850, achieving particular success with photographs of moving humans, trotting horses and waves.

MACPHERSON, Robert (1811–72)

Scottish surgeon, painter, topographical and copy photographer.

Settled in Rome in the early 1840s.

Active in photography from the early 1850s, recording and copying the Roman antiquities, architecture and sculpture; often as large format photographs for mass sale in London and elsewhere.

Published in 1863 *Guidebook to Sculpture in the Vatican*.

MADDOX, Richard Leach (1816–1902)

English doctor and photo-chemist.

Suggested in 1871 the use of gelatin emulsion, instead of wet collodion, for photographic plates. The suggestion was swiftly taken up and developed to become the basis of the Dry Plate process.

MANLY, Thomas (died 1932)

English photographer and photographic inventor.

Introduced in 1899 the Ozotype process and, in 1905, the Ozobrome process.

MANN, F. S.

English topographical photographer.

Active from Hastings, Sussex, during the second half of the nineteenth century.

MANSELL, Thomas L.

English landscape and topographical photographer.

Active from the early 1850s in France and England, producing notably sharp quality photographs, many of rocks and foliage.

MAREY, Etienne Jules (1830–1904)

French physiologist and motion photographer.

From *circa* 1882 investigated human and animal movement with a single camera and revolving disc shutter.

Published, with Georges Demeny, in 1893 in several parts *Etude de Physiologie Artistique. Des Mouvements de L'homme.*

Illustration—179.

MARION and COMPANY
(MARION, A.)

French portrait photographers, photographic publishers, print and photographic merchants.

Based in London during the second half of the nineteenth century, handling many millions of carte-de-visite and cabinet portrait photographs and similar material.

MARTIN, Adolphe Alexandre (1824–86)
French photographic inventor.
Introduced in 1852/3 the Ferrotype or Tintype process.

MARTIN, Paul (1864–1942)
English wood engraver, illustrative and genre photographer.
Active in photography from the late 1880s, particularly with straight, snapshot-like photographs of London street scenes, the tradesmen and the poor, and the Yarmouth, Norfolk, seaside.
During 1895–6 Paul Martin made a series of photographs of 'London by Night'.
Published in 1939 *Victorian Snapshots*, his autobiography.
Prints may be signed with his name impressed on the card mounts.
Illustrations—184, 185, 186, 187 and 188.

MARVILLE, Charles
French graphic and lithographic artist and topographical photographer.
Active in Paris during the 1850s, 60s and 70s, particularly in recording the buildings, monuments and architecture. Also the ruins of the Hôtel de Ville after the fire in 1871.
Illustrations—114 and 115.

MAULL and COMPANY
(MAULL and FOX)
(MAULL and POLYBLANK)
Apparently the same basic firm but with different partnerships.
English portrait photographers.

London studios from the 1850s, at 55 Gracechurch Street and 187a Piccadilly.
Illustration—66.

MAXWELL, Sir James Clerk (1831–79)
Scottish mathematician, physicist and pioneer of colour photography.
Demonstrated in 1861 the first colour photography, producing a projected image of a tartan-ribbon, based on the Additive System.

MAY, William
English topographical photographer.
Active from Devonport, Devon, during the second half of the nineteenth century.

MAYALL, John Jabez Edwin (1810–1901)
American daguerreotype and portrait photographer.
Daguerreotype studio, with Marcus A. Root, in Philadelphia from 1842 to 1846.
In 1847 Mayall moved to England, opening the 'American Daguerreotype Institution' in London at 433 West Strand, apparently partly using the pseudonym 'Professor Highschool'.
His daguerreotype activities included a series of 10 photographs illustrating the Lord's Prayer, in 1845, and a collection of large format art daguerreotypes for the Great Exhibition of 1851.
Later, at 224 Regent Street, London, and with an extra studio at Brighton, Sussex, Mayall turned to carte-de-visite and, finally, cabinet portrait photography; ranking amongst the most successful and most active commercial portrait photographers of the nineteenth century.
Illustrations—61, 62, and 64.

MAYBERRY, J. H.
American portrait, genre, topographical and landscape photographer.

Active from New Castle, Wyoming, during the second half of the nineteenth century, notably with straight reportage photographs of the rough and tough American western life, the miners and cow punchers.

Illustrations—139 and 140.

MAYLAND, W.

English landscape and topographical photographer.

Active in Cambridge during the middle of the nineteenth century.

Exhibited series of photographs of Cambridge Colleges, cloisters and interiors, in the Exhibition of 1862.

MÉLANDRI

French portrait photographer.

Active in Paris during the 1860s and 70s.

Illustration—56.

MELHUISH, Arthur James (died 1895)

English portrait photographer and photographic inventor.

Studio in London.

With J. B. Spencer, in 1854, invented a very early kind of roll film involving sensitized waxed paper.

MENDELSSOHN, H. S.

English portrait photographer.

Studios in London and Newcastle-on-Tyne during the second half of the nineteenth century and early twentieth century, particularly for carte-de-visite and cabinet portrait photography.

MISONNE, Léonard (1870–1943)

Belgian artist photographer.

Active from circa 1895, and well into the mid twentieth century.

MOFFAT, J. (died 1894)

Scottish portrait photographer.

Active from 1853.

Studio at 103 Princes Street, Edinburgh.

Produced a well known series of carte-de-visite portraits of William Henry Fox Talbot.

Illustration—78.

MORA, José Maria (born 1849)

American (Cuban born) portrait photographer.

Studio at 707 Broadway, New York, for carte-de-visite and cabinet portrait photography, from 1870.

Illustration—159.

MORSE, G. D.

American portrait photographer.

Studio—'Morse's Palace of Art'—at 417 Montgomery Street, San Francisco, during the latter part of the nineteenth century.

MORSE, Samuel Finley Breese (1791–1872)

American telegraphic inventor and early daguerreotype photographer.

Inventor of the Morse Code.

Opened a portrait studio at New York University with Dr. John W. Draper in the spring of 1840.

MUDD, James

English textile designer, portrait and landscape photographer.

Active in Manchester during the 1850s and 60s.

Recorded the dam burst disaster at Sheffield in 1864.

MUYBRIDGE, Eadweard James (1830–1904)

English topographical and motion photographer.

During the late 1860s and early 1870s photographed topography and landscape in America; some for railway and steamship companies.

From 1872 investigated human and animal movement, with all sorts of different beasts, birds and humans (including some with malformations) before rows of small cameras.

In 1877 Muybridge made the first successful photographs of horses in motion, destroying all earlier theories on the manner in which they move.

Published in 1887 *Animal Locomotion*, photogravures of his work from 1872 to 1885.

Illustrations—174, 175 and 176.

NADAR (1820–1910). Pseudonym of Gaspard Félix TOURNACHON

French caricaturist, writer, balloonist, topographical and portrait photographer.

Portrait studio, with his brother, in Rue St. Lazare, Paris, from 1853. Second studio in Boulevard des Capucines, Paris, from 1860, was painted red overall, with an outsize signature, also in red, across the façade. Later studio in Rue d'Anjou, Paris.

Nadar's portraits, strong and dramatic, are among the finest of any period. He photographed extravagantly—writers, artists, nobility and all.

In 1858 he took the first ever aerial photographs—from his balloon.

In 1860 he photographed the catacombs and sewers of Paris—by electric light.

In 1886 he introduced the photo-interview —a series of portrait photographs accompanied by appropriate extracts of conversation.

Published in 1899 *Quand J'étais Photographe*, his autobiography.

'Connaissez vous Nadar? Non. C'est dommage, Madame, c'est encore un bel homme. Il a six pieds de haut, une tête gauloise avec des moustiches belliqueuses' (*Les Hommes d'Aujourd'hui*, November 1878).

With hair as red as his studio Nadar was one of the grand and colourful characters of early photography.

Prints may be signed boldly in the plate, in red, or sometimes stamped with his name.

Illustrations—57, 74 and 75.

NADAR, Paul (1856–1939)

French portrait photographer.

The son of Nadar.

Active in Paris, particularly with 'At Home' portraiture.

Illustration—180.

NAYA, C.

Italian topographical and copy photographer.

Very active in Venice during the second half of the nineteenth century, recording the architecture, topography, sculpture and paintings.

Contributed to *Ricordo di Venezia*, albums of photographs published by Carlo Ponti.

NEALE, Arthur

English portrait photographer.

Studio in Nottingham during the latter part of the nineteenth century.

NÈGRE, Charles (1820–c. 1880)

French painter, portrait, genre, landscape and topographical photographer and photographic inventor.

Engaged in photography from 1851, achieving great success with genre subjects, chimney sweeps' boys, tinkers, organ grinders and so forth, as well as some very fine photographs of architecture.

Portrait studio in Paris.

Invented *circa* 1860 a kind of photo-engraving process on steel.

Prints may be signed in the plate.

NEGRETTI (Henry 1818–c. 1879) and ZAMBRA (Joseph born 1822)

Italian born, London based, scientific instrument and camera manufacturers, merchants, portrait and topographical photographers.

Founded in 1850, Negretti and Zambra developed into one of the most active and diversified photographic firms of any period. Their activities were many and various:

Official photographers to the Crystal Palace Company;

Several studios, in London and at the Crystal Palace, for carte-de-visite and cabinet portrait photography;

Manufacturers of every kind of photographic equipment and device, as well as magic and phantasmagoria lanterns;

In May 1863 Henry Negretti became the first person to take photographs of London from the air—in a specially fitted balloon;

and, rumour rumbles,

Suppliers of shepherds, complete with dogs, to Patagonia.

The firm remains in active business.

Illustrations—91 and 92.

NEURDEIN, E.
(NEURDEIN FRÈRES—from *circa* 1892)

French topographical photographer/s.

Based in Paris but widely active in Europe (notably Switzerland in 1891) recording views, sculpture and architecture—frequently as large format panoramas—during the second half of the nineteenth century.

Illustrations—152, 177 and 178.

NIÉPCE, Claude (1763–1828)

French naval officer and pioneer of photography.

The brother of Nicéphore Niépce and one time colleague in their earliest attempts to fix the camera's image.

NIÉPCE, Isidore (1805–68)

French photographic inventor.

The son of Nicéphore Niépce.

When his father died in 1833 Isidore continued the partnership with L. J. M. Daguerre.

On the announcement of the daguerreotype process, in 1839, he was awarded a pension by the French government, although his part in the invention may have been very small.

NIÉPCE, Joseph Nicéphore (1765–1833)

French landowner, army officer and inventor of photography.

A rich gentleman and an ex-officer in the French army Nicéphore Niépce began his experiments to fix the images made by the camera obscura in about 1815/6.

During the 1820s, at his home near Châlon-sur-Saône, he took and fixed the first successful photographs ever.

Using exposures as long as 8 hours and metal (zinc, pewter or silvered copper) or glass plates coated with bitumen of Judea, which hardens on exposure to light, he fixed his images by washing away the less hardened area of bitumen with a solvent of oil of lavender and petroleum. The final picture, Heliograph, being formed by the bitumen in varying thicknesses and the exposed surface of the plate.

Niépce's original intention had been to make plates for printing from along lithographic lines, and several heliographs of old engravings were made for this purpose.

The earliest heliograph, photograph, from nature still known to exist, the view from an upstairs window of his home, he took in 1826 on a pewter plate coated with bitumen of Judea. Another heliograph from nature, showing a table laid for a meal, but made on glass, has long since been lost or destroyed, but a copy remains and it has been claimed that this dates from as early as 1822. This may be so, but nothing is completely certain and 1829, another suggested date, could be more accurate.

From 1829 he collaborated with L. J. M. Daguerre. A partnership which was to result in the invention and announcement of the Daguerreotype process in 1839, although Niépce himself had died in 1833.

Illustrations—1 and 2.

NIÉPCE de SAINT VICTOR, Claude Félix Abel (1805–70)

French soldier, scientist and photographic inventor.

The cousin of Nicéphore Niépce.

Introduced in 1848 the Albumen on Glass process.

Founder member of the Société Héliographique, 1851.

NOTMAN, William (1826–91)

British born portrait, genre and landscape photographer.

Active in Canada from the mid 1850s, with studios in Montreal, Ottawa, Toronto and Halifax, Nova Scotia, achieving special success with collective portraits of the indigenous Canadians, Indians, hunters and trappers, as well as settled dignitaries.

Later formed the Notman Photographic Company, with studios in New York and Boston, Massachusetts.

Illustrations—134, 135, 136 and 137.

NUNN, F.

English seaside portrait photographer.

Active from 1869 in Scarborough, Yorkshire, at The Children's Corner, South Sands.

Employed the ambrotype process.

Illustration—167.

OGLE, T.

Scottish(?) topographical and landscape photographer.

One time partnership with –. Edge for the publication of stereoscope slides of English topography.

Illustrated Sir Walter Scott's *The Lady of the Lake*, 1863, and contributed to the 1864 edition of William and Mary Howitt's *Ruined Abbeys and Castles of Great Britain and Ireland*.

O'SULLIVAN, Timothy H. (*c*. 1840–82)

American portrait, war and topographical photographer.

Initially with Mathew B. Brady in studios in New York and Washington, Timothy H. O'Sullivan became, like Alexander Gardner, a prominent member of the team of photographers organized to record the American Civil War, 1861–5.

Later, between 1867 and 1873, he accompanied several American government surveys and expeditions—to the 40th Parallel, to the Isthmus of Darien (a survey for the Panama canal), to the Colorado River and to Arizona. He produced some exceptionally fine and majestic photographs of mountains and canyons, lakes and rivers.

Finally official photographer to the Treasury Department, Washington.

Illustrations—72 and 138.

PATTISON, Rev. James Whitehead (1853–1936)

English clergyman and part time genre photographer.

Active in photography from *circa* 1885, producing straight, simple photographs of the everyday life in the parishes with which he was connected. Beach scenes, trades people, fisher people, the ordinary working men, women and children of north-east England, particularly Seaton and Hartlepool, and then from 1906, Weardale.

Illustrations—191, 192, 193, 194, 195 and 196.

PECK, Samuel
(SAMUEL PECK and COMPANY)

American daguerreotype photographer and photograph case manufacturer.

Patented American Union in October 1854.

PICKERSGILL, Frederick Richard (1820–1900)

English genre painter, landscape and topographical photographer.

Contributed to *The Sunbeam*, 1859, a book of photographs edited by P. H. Delamotte—under his own name and the pseudonym 'Phoebus'.

PIPER, C. Welborne (1866–1919)

English photographer and photographic inventor.

With E. J. Wall, introduced the Bromoil process in 1907.

PIPER, John Dixon

English topographical and landscape photographer.

Active during the middle of the nineteenth century.

PLUMBE, John (1811–57)

Welsh born daguerreotype photographer and manufacturer of materials.

Active in America during the 1840s and 50s with more than 12 studios across the country.

POITEVIN, Alphonse Louis (1819–82)

French chemist, photographer and photographic inventor.

Introduced in 1855 the Collotype process and Carbon Print process.

POLAK, Richard (born 1870)

American 'pictorial' photographer.

Renowned for extraordinary imitations of seventeenth century Dutch paintings, made during the early twentieth century.

Illustration—252.

PONTI, Carlo

Italian genre and topographical photographer.

Active during the 1850s and 60s, specializing in photographs of North Italian cities.

Invented, *circa* 1860, the Megalethoscope, a kind of large panoramic photograph viewer.

Published during the 1860s several albums entitled *Ricordo di Venezia*.

Illustration—96.

POULTON, S.

English portrait and topographical photographer.

Active during the second half of the nineteenth century publishing views in series, frequently as stereoscope slides.

London studio at 252 Strand.

Illustrated the Imperial edition of *The Poetical Works of Sir Walter Scott*, *circa* 1880.

POUNCY, John (died 1894)

English portrait, landscape and topographical photographer and photographic inventor.

Studio in Dorchester, Dorset, during the second half of the nineteenth century.

Pioneered several photographic printing processes, including the carbon print.

Published in 1857 *Dorset Photographically Illustrated*, an album of pictures produced by a lithographic process from photographs.

Illustration—181.

PRETSCH, Paul (1808–73)

Austrian portrait, genre and landscape photographer and photographic inventor.

Active in Vienna and then, from 1854 to 1863, in England.

Invented several photographic printing and engraving processes, including, in 1854, Photogalvanography—a pioneering photo-mechanical printing process.

PRICE, William Lake (1810–96)

English watercolour artist, topographical, portrait, copy and artist photographer.

A leading watercolour painter, engaged in photography from 1854 to circa 1862, William Lake Price became one of the first to make combination photographs—pictures made up from several different negatives.

Roman topography and copy photography of old master paintings, formed the two other major parts of his photographic activity.

PUYO, Emile Joachim Constant (1857–1933)

French army officer and artist photographer.

Active during the late nineteenth and early twentieth centuries, generally employing the gum print process for photographs of an impressionistic nature.

Illustration—235.

RABENDING (Emil 1823–86) and van MONCKHOVEN (Désiré Charles Emanuel 1834–82)

Austrian and Belgian portrait photographers.

In partnership in Vienna from the late 1860s.

REGNAULT, Henri Victor (1810–78)

French engineer, scientist, calotype, portrait and topographical photographer.

Active in photography from the 1840s, particularly with especially sensitive and gentle portraits and landscapes.

Founder member of the Société Héliographique, 1851.

Director of the Sèvres porcelain factory, 1854.

Illustration—30.

REJLANDER, Oscar Gustave (1813–75)

Swedish painter, portrait, genre and artist photographer.

Settled in England in the 1840s, with a portrait studio in Wolverhampton from circa 1855.

In London from 1860.

Celebrated in early photography for his genre subjects and grand, original and elaborate pictorial photographs—especially 'The Two Ways of Life', 1857, a photograph made up from over 30 different negatives.

Contributed to Charles Darwin's The Expressions of the Emotions in Man and Animals, 1872.

An imposing figure and character, Oscar Rejlander is rumoured to have judged exposures by the eyes of his pet cat. He died in poverty.

Illustrations—43 and 44.

REUTLINGER, Ch.

French portrait photographer.

Studio in Paris, 21 Boulevard Montmartre, during the second half of the nineteenth century.

Illustration—58.

RIIS, Jacob A. (1849–1914)

Danish born American news reporter and sociological photographer.

Police court reporter on the New York Tribune from 1877.

From 1887 to 1892 Jacob Riis photographed the slums of New York.

Published in 1890 How the Other Half Lives and in 1892 Children of the Poor.

The Jacob A. Riis Neighbourhood Settlement, a rebuilt area of New York, carries his name in recognition of his photographic exposé of the conditions previously existing in slum tenements.

Illustration—205.

ROBERT, Paul

French topographical photographer.

Active in Paris during the end of the nineteenth century, with photographic records of the architecture, streets and shop fronts.

ROBERTSON, James

British medal designer, landscape, topographical and war photographer.

Active from the early 1850s, publishing views of the Mediterranean and Near Eastern countries, islands and cities.

In 1855–6 photographed in the Crimea during the close of the war.

With Felice A. Beato he travelled and photographed in Palestine and Syria in 1857; later covering the Indian Mutiny, 1857–8.

Prints may be signed, in the plate or on the finished print, with his surname alone.

Illustrations—35 and 36.

ROBINSON, Henry Peach (1830–1901)

English bookshop assistant, painter, portrait and artist photographer.

Portrait studio in Leamington from January 1857. In 1868 he moved to Tunbridge Wells where he was in partnership with N. K. Cherrill.

Henry Peach Robinson became well known for his combination photographs—pictures made up from several different negatives based on preliminary sketches—with such titles as 'Fading Away' (1858), 'When Day's Work is Done' (1877), 'Wayside Gossip' (1883) and 'Dawn and Sunset' (1885), mounted and framed as oil paintings and frequently accompanied by appropriate verse.

Published in 1869 *Pictorial Effect in Photography* and in 1884 *Picture Making by Photography*.

Founder member of the Linked Ring Brotherhood, 1892.

Illustrations—45, 46 and 47.

ROOT, Marcus A.

American painter, writer and daguerreotype photographer.

In partnership with J. J. E. Mayall in Philadelphia, 1842–6.

Published in 1864 *The Camera and the Pencil*.

ROSS (James) and THOMSON (John)

Scottish daguerreotype, landscape and portrait photographers.

Active in Edinburgh during the second half of the nineteenth century, achieving special success with portraits of small children.

de ROSTI, Paul (1830–74)

Hungarian topographical photographer.

Travelled and photographed in Mexico, *circa* 1860.

de la RUE, Warren (1815–89)

English chemist, astronomer and celestial photographer.

Engaged in photography from 1852, with the moon in 1857, sunspots in 1861, and other heavenly bodies. Stereoscope slides on glass were subsequently published by Smith, Beck and Beck, London.

RUSSELL, Charles (1820–87)

English army officer, photographer and photographic inventor.

Introduced in 1861 the Tannin process.

SARONY, Napoleon (1821–96)

Canadian born painter and portrait photographer.

The brother of Olivier Sarony.

Studio in Birmingham, England, with S. Laroche, from 1864 to 1866.

In 1866 opened the first of several studios in New York, achieving most recognition with cabinet portrait photography.

Illustration—69.

SARONY, Olivier Francois Xavier (1820–79)

Canadian born portrait photographer and photographic inventor.

The brother of Napoleon Sarony.

Studios in London and, from 1857, Scarborough where his success and popularity were such that a square was named after him.

Developed in the early 1870s a special enlarging technique.

Illustration—83.

SAVAGE, W.

English topographical photographer.

Active in Winchester, Hampshire, during the second half of the nineteenth century.

Illustrated *Memorials of the Hospital of Saint Cross*, 1868.

SAWYER, J. R.
(SAWYER and BIRD)

English portrait photographer/s.

Very active in carte-de-visite and cabinet portrait photography during the 1860s, 70s and early 80s, with studios in Norfolk (Norwich and Yarmouth) and London.

Later, *circa* 1883, the firm was taken over by Albert E. Coe.

SAWYER, Lyddell (born 1856)

English portrait, genre and topographical photographer.

From the early 1870s Lyddell Sawyer worked in his father's studio at Newcastle-on-Tyne. Later he opened his own studios: in Sunderland in 1893 and in Regent Street, London, in 1895.

Between times he produced sensitive and gentle naturalistic photographs, landscapes and genre subjects.

Founder member of the Linked Ring Brotherhood, 1892.

Illustration—237.

SEAGER, D. W.

English born daguerreotype photographer.

Took the first daguerreotype in America, a view of St. Paul's Church, New York, on 16 September 1839.

SEDGEFIELD, W. Russell

English topographical photographer.

Active *circa* 1842 to 1872.

Published *Sedgefield's English Scenery*—an extensive series of stereoscope slides.

Contributed to both editions of William and Mary Howitt's *Ruined Abbeys and Castles of Great Britain and Ireland*, 1862 and 1864.

SELLA, Vittorio (1859–1943)

Italian topographical photographer.

Active during the end of the nineteenth and early twentieth centuries, particularly with mountain photography.

SHEPHERD, –.
(BOURNE and SHEPHERD)

English(?) portrait and topographical photographer.

Active in India during the second half of the nineteenth century.

Studio partnership with Samuel Bourne at Simla, Calcutta and Bombay.

Illustrated Henry Hardy Cole's *The Architecture of Ancient Delhi Especially the Buildings Around the Kutb Minar*, 1872.

Illustration—88.

SHIMOOKA, Renjo (1825–1914)

Japanese portrait photographer.

Active in Yokohama from 1862.

SILVY, Camille

French aristocrat, landscape and portrait photographer.

During the 1850s Camille Silvy produced exceptionally fine landscape photographs, neatly finished, boldly and precisely signed.

Portrait studio in Porchester Terrace, London, from 1859 to 1869, for probably the finest of all carte-de-visite photography.

Published a series of carte-de-visite portraits entitled *The Beauties of England*.

Later studio in the suburbs of Paris.

Illustrations—48 and 49.

SMITH (Frederick B.) and HARTMANN (Herman)

American engravers and diesinkers.

Active in New York during the 1850s, with designs for American Union cases.

SMITH, John Shaw (1811–73)

Irish landscape and topographical photographer.

Active during the 1850s, producing photographs from his travels in Europe and the Middle East.

SMITH, Lyndon

English landscape photographer.

Active in Leeds, Yorkshire, during the middle of the nineteenth century.

Exhibited series of landscape photographs 'artistically taken' at the Exhibition of 1862.

SMYTH, Charles Piazzi (1819–1900)

Scottish astronomer, topographical and astronomical photographer.

Photographed the interior of the Great Pyramid in 1865.

Published in 1858 *Teneriffe: An Astronomer's Experiment, or Specialities of a Residence Above the Clouds*, the first publication illustrated by stereoscopic photographs.

SOMMER, Giorgio
(G. SOMMER and FIGLIO)

Italian genre and topographical photographer/s.

Studio in Naples, during the late nineteenth century, producing topographical views, mainly of Italy, for sale in collections in album form.

Illustration—157.

SOULIER, Charles

French topographical photographer.

Active during the second half of the nineteenth century, particularly with very fine views of Mont Blanc, French and Swiss topography, Roman architecture and sculpture; many, taken in partnership with the Ferriers, père et fils, for publication as stereoscope slides on glass.

Slides may be signed with his initials, in the plate.

Illustrations—150 and 151.

SOUTHWORTH (Albert Sands 1811–94) and HAWES (Josiah John★ died 1901)

American daguerreotype, portrait and landscape photographers.

Studio in Boston, Massachusetts, from *circa* 1850.

(★ Johnson is also recorded as his second Christian name.)

de ST. CROIX, M.

French daguerreotype agent and photographer.

In England from September 1839 with examples of French daguerreotypes and with demonstrations of the process in recording London topography.

STEICHEN, Edward (born 1879)

American painter, portrait, artist and fashion photographer.

Active in photography from 1896, exhibiting, at first, gum print and other controlled process photographs.

One man exhibition in Paris in 1902.

Founder member of Photo-Secession, 1902.

With Alfred Stieglitz in 1905 he started the Photo-Secession Gallery, 291 Fifth Avenue, New York; later known as the '291'.

Following the First World War Steichen turned completely from his earlier controlled print processes to straight, pure, photography.

Later, during the 1920s and 30s, he became fashion photographer for Condé Nast publications. Then, from 1947, curator of photography at the Museum of Modern Art, New York.

Published in 1963 *A Life in Photography*.

Illustration—241.

STELZNER, Carl Ferdinand (*c.* 1805–94)

German miniature painter and daguerreotype photographer.

From 1842 in partnership with Hermann Biow, at Hamburg, photographing in May the same year the ruins left by a fire in the city—the earliest news photographs.

STEPHENS, John Lloyd

American explorer and topographical photographer.

With Frederick Catherwood, in 1841, made daguerreotype records of the 'lost cities' of Yucatan.

STEWART, John

English calotype, topographical and portrait photographer.

The son-in-law of Sir John Herschel.

Widely active, particularly in Europe, Spain and France in the 1850s, 60s and 70s.

STIEGLITZ, Alfred (1864–1946)

American portrait, genre and artist photographer.

Alfred Stieglitz achieved early success with a very memorable, well known series of straight photographs of everyday life in the centre of New York taken, from 1892, in deliberately chosen adverse conditions of snow and storm, rain, mist and smoke.

Principal founding member of Photo-Secession, 1902.

Founder, in 1905, and director of the Photo-Secession Gallery, 291 Fifth Avenue, New York; later known as the '291'.

Editor of *Camera Work* magazine, 1903 to 1917—probably the finest photographic magazine there has ever been.

Stieglitz was the prime advocate of straight, pure photography, against the manipulated and controlled print processes popular at the turn of the century.

Illustrations—238, 239 and 240.

STODDARD, S. R.

American topographical photographer.

Active from Glen Falls, New York, during the second half of the nineteenth century.

Illustration—131.

STONE, Sir Benjamin (1838–1914)

English business man, politician, genre and portrait photographer.

Conservative member of Parliament for Birmingham.

Prolific in photography, Benjamin Stone produced close on 30,000 photographs of the declining and disappearing activities of English life, fairs and festivals, ox-roastings and may dancing, besides records of the ceremonies of Parliament.

Founder of the National Photographic Record Association, for the documentation of 'old manners and customs', 1895.

Published in 1905 *Sir Benjamin Stone's Pictures* (2 volumes).

Illustration—183.

STROHMEYER and WYMAN

American photographic publishers.

Active in New York from the end of the

nineteenth century, publishing series of stereoscope slides.

Illustration—132.

SUTCLIFFE, Frank Meadows (1853–1941)

English portrait, genre and landscape photographer.

Active at Whitby, Yorkshire, from 1875—commercially with carte-de-visite and cabinet portrait photography, but artistically with some of the finest, straight and natural photography produced in the nineteenth century.

Frank Meadows Sutcliffe concentrated on photographing life in and around the farming areas and fishing ports of Yorkshire in a subtle and simple style.

Founder member of the Linked Ring Brotherhood, 1892.

Retired from photography in 1922.

Prints are generally signed or inscribed with his initials and a reference number.

Illustrations—80, 213, 214, 215 and 216.

SWAN, Sir Joseph Wilson (1828–1914)

English scientist, photographic inventor and manufacturer.

Perfected in 1864 the Carbon Print process.

TABER, I. W.

American portrait and topographical photographer

Studio in San Francisco during the second half of the nineteenth century, particularly for cabinet portrait photography.

TALBOT, William Henry Fox (1800–77)

English landowner, scientist, inventor of photography and calotype photographer.

A rich country gentleman and member of Parliament with his seat at Lacock Abbey, Wiltshire, Talbot experimented with photography from 1833; endeavouring to capture the image made by the camera obscura on paper sensitized with silver nitrate and common salt. In August 1835 he produced the earliest surviving negative—of a window at Lacock Abbey.

Learning of Daguerre's achievement, in 1839, he published his own negative and positive process on paper—Photogenic Drawing. During 1840 he greatly speeded up and improved the process when he discovered that a latent image on the paper could be brought out, developed, with gallo nitrate of silver, after an exposure of only 2 or 3 minutes against the hour previously required. This new method, the Calotype or Talbotype process he published and patented in 1841.

From 1843 to 1847 Talbot was active from his establishment at Reading, Berkshire, producing portraits, genre, landscape and topographical photographs, assisted by Nicolaas Henneman.

As a copy photographer he contributed 66 calotypes of Spanish paintings and prints to Sir William Stirling Maxwell's *Annals of the Artists of Spain*, published in 4 volumes in 1847.

Later, *circa* 1858, he developed Photoglyphic Engraving—a pioneering photographic engraving process.

Published between 1844 and 1846 *The Pencil of Nature* and in 1845 *Sun Pictures of Scotland*.

William Henry Fox Talbot's calotypes of chess players and the construction of Nelson's column in Trafalgar Square, and his photomicrographs of butterfly wings, are among the great rarities and wonders of early photography.

Illustrations—11, 12, 13, 14, 15 and 16.

TAMOTO, K.

Japanese portrait photographer.

Studio in Hakodate, Japan, during the close of the nineteenth century, for carte-de-visite and cabinet portrait photography.

Illustration—94.

TAYLOR, A. and G.

English portrait photographers.

Active during the second half of the nineteenth century with carte-de-visite and cabinet portrait photography.

Claimed to be 'The Largest Photographers in the World'.

Studios at 153 Regent Street, London, throughout the British Isles and in America.

Illustrations—164, 165 and 169.

TAYLOR, T.

English portrait photographer.

Employed the ferrotype process in studios at Halifax and Bradford, Yorkshire, during the end of the nineteenth century.

Advertised as an 'American Gem Photographer. 9 correct portraits for $7\frac{1}{2}d$. While you wait'.

Illustration—171.

THOMPSON, C. Thurston (died 1867)

English military, topographical and copy photographer.

Copy photographed the Raphael cartoons for illustrations to a guide book by R. H. Smith, published in 1861.

THOMPSON, S.

English(?) topographical photographer.

Contributed to the 1864 edition of William and Mary Howitt's *Ruined Abbeys and Castles of Great Britain and Ireland*.

THOMSON, John (1837–1921)

Scottish traveller, topographical, genre and portrait photographer.

Active from the mid 1860s—initially travelling and recording topography in the Far East.

In England during the 1870s John Thomson took a rare series of photographs of the ordinary street and working class life of London. With the help of the writer, Adolphe Smith, these were published as woodburytypes with texts in 6 parts, during 1877, under the title *Street Life in London*.

Other publications include *Antiquities of Cambodia*, 1867, *Illustrations of China and its People*, 1873, and *Through Cyprus with the Camera*, 1878.

Later portrait studio at 70a Grosvenor Street, London, busy into the twentieth century.

Illustrations—118 and 119.

TURNER, Benjamin Bracknell (1815–94)

English painter, calotype and landscape photographer.

Active in photography during the 1840s, 50s and 60s, with fine, high quality landscapes. He may have assisted William Henry Fox Talbot with *The Pencil of Nature*, 1844–6.

TURNER and DRINKWATER

English portrait photographers.

Studios in London and Hull during the second half of the nineteenth century.

Illustration—160.

UENO, Toshinojo

Japanese chemist and daguerreotype photographer.

Probably the first photographer in Japan—active from *circa* 1840/1 at Nagasaki.

UNDERWOOD and UNDERWOOD

American stereoscope photographers and photographic publishers.

Very active during the close of the nineteenth century and early twentieth century with branches in America, Canada and England, producing series and collections of stereoscope slides; generally fully marked with their name and copyright date.

VALENTINE, James (1815–80)

Scottish topographical and landscape photographer.

Based at Dundee, though very active very widely, producing vast numbers of consistently fine topographical photographs, often rendered the more interesting by the inclusion of figures.

Prints are frequently titled and marked with his initials, although many were taken by his assistants and not by he himself.

Illustration—141.

de VILLENEUVE, Julien Vallou

French painter, lithographic artist and nude photographer.

Active in photography from the early 1840s, especially with the female nude—publishing series of prints intended primarily as aids to painters.

Prints are generally signed in the plate, in full or in monogram.

Illustrations—27, 28 and 29.

VOIGTLÄNDER, Peter Wilhelm Friedrich (1812–78)

Austrian optical instrument and camera manufacturer.

In 1841 produced the first all metal camera. Incorporating the fast lens calculated by Josef Petzval this cone shape camera formed a major contribution to the daguerreotype process in reducing the time required to make an exposure.

WALKER, Samuel A.

English portrait photographer.

Studio in Regent Street, London, from the second half of the nineteenth century for carte-de-visite and cabinet portrait photography especially and, later, 'At Home' photography.

'Portraits of ladies, children and laymen as well as the clergy are taken daily at this studio, also photographs of every description.' (Cabinet portrait reverse.)

WALKER, S. L.

American daguerreotype photographer.

Studio at Poughkeepsie, New York, during the 1850s.

WALL, Edward John (1860–1928)

English writer, chemist, photographer and photographic inventor.

With C. Welborne Piper, introduced the Bromoil process in 1907.

Published in 1889 *Dictionary of Photography*.

WALLER, J.

English portrait and landscape photographer.

Active in Whitby, Yorkshire, during the second half of the nineteenth century.

WATKINS, Carleton E. (died 1916)

American topographical photographer.

Active during the second half of the nineteenth century.

WATKINS, Herbert

English portrait photographer.

Studio in London during the second half of the nineteenth century.

WATZEK, Hans (1848–1903)

Austrian impressionistic photographer.

Active in Vienna during the late nineteenth

century, generally using controlled print processes for portraits, landscapes and still life photographs.

Illustration—231.

WHEATSTONE, Sir Charles (1802–75)

English scientist and Stereoscope inventor.

From 1832 to 1838 developed the stereoscope for geometric designs and then, *circa* 1845, for photography.

WHITE, Clarence Hudson (1871–1925)

American artist photographer.

Active from the mid 1890s.

Produced straight portrait and landscape photographs, often taken into the light to give a chiaroscuro character and to reveal 'a mind unusually sensitive to the glory of light' (*New York Times*).

Founder member of Photo-Secession, 1902.

Illustrations—246 and 247.

WHITE, Henry (1819–1903)

English solicitor and landscape photographer.

Active during 1850s and 60s, producing landscape photographs and, *circa* 1857, an especially fine close up of brambles and ivy.

WILKINSON, Benjamin Gay (1857–1927)

English solicitor and naturalistic landscape photographer.

Active from *circa* 1875.

Founder member of the Linked Ring Brotherhood, 1892.

Illustration—222.

WILLIS, William (1841–1923)

English bank clerk, engineer, photographer and photographic inventor.

Patented in 1873 the Platinotype process.

Founded in 1878 the Platinotype Company for the manufacture of platinum printing paper.

WILSON, Charles A. (1865–1958)

Scottish topographical and genre photographer.

The son of George Washington Wilson.

Photographed London street scenes from the inside of a furniture van, *circa* 1887.

WILSON, George Washington (1823–93)

Scottish landscape, topographical and portrait photographer.

Established at Aberdeen in 1852, though active very widely with consistently fine photography—single prints, series, stereoscope slides and cartes-de-visite.

Books with George Washington Wilson's photographs as illustrations include *The Sunbeam*, 1859; the 1862 edition of William and Mary Howitt's *Ruined Abbeys and Castles of Great Britain and Ireland*; and Sir Walter Scott's *Poetical Works*, 1886.

Prints are generally titled and marked with his initials, although many were actually taken by his assistants and not by he himself.

Illustrations—142, 143 and 182.

WOLCOTT, Alexander S. (1804–44)

American daguerreotype photographer.

With his partner, John Johnson, the first in the world to open a photographic studio, a 'Daguerrian Parlor', in New York early in March 1840.

Patented in May 1840 a special daguerreotype camera in which a concave mirror replaced the lens—a device which shortened the length of time then required for an exposure.

WOODBURY, Francis
(WOODBURY and PAGE)

Australian born explorer, portrait and topographical photographer.

Active in Java during the 1850s and 60s.

Studio partnership with –. Page, in Djakarta.

Stereoscope slides on glass of Java were published in England by Negretti and Zambra.

WOODBURY, Walter Bentley (1834–85)

English photographer and photographic inventor.

Introduced in 1864/5 the Woodburytype process.

WRIGGLESWORTH and BINNS

New Zealand portrait and genre photographers.

Active from Wellington, New Zealand, during the second half of the nineteenth century, particularly with genre photographs of the Maori people.

WYNFIELD, David Wilkie (1837–87)

English historical painter and portrait photographer.

Made a rare series of portraits of fellow painters, many of them in fancy dress, including Holman Hunt, Lord Leighton and Millais.

General Information, the Types of Photography, the Processes

A negative and positive photographic process on glass.

Introduced by Abel Niépce de Saint Victor in June 1848.

Glass was coated with albumen (from the white of egg) and potassium iodide and then sensitized with an acid solution of silver nitrate. Following exposure the latent image was developed with gallic acid.

The results gave exceptionally fine definition and the process was therefore well suited to topographical photography and lantern slides—but, due to the long exposures required, it was not so suitable for portrait or figure subjects.

ALBUMEN PRINT

The main type of paper print in use during the second half of the nineteenth century.

Introduced by L. D. Blanquart-Evrard in May 1850.

From *circa* 1860 the paper could be bought in a semi-prepared state, ready coated with albumen (from the white of egg) and salt. This was sensitized before use with a solution of silver nitrate.

The resultant print was usually sepia toned (with chloride of gold) to avoid quick fading and to disguise the unattractive yellow colour of the raw print.

AMBROTYPE

A wet collodion 'positive' on glass.

Developed by Frederick Scott Archer and P. W. Fry, *circa* 1851.

A popular method of small portrait, and subject, photography during the 1850s and 60s, although in use for many years later.

A glass negative image was bleached, with nitric acid or bichloride of mercury, and then laid against a black background to give a positive picture. When finished the photograph was generally mounted in a frame, folder or case—sometimes of American Union.

As the sole negative was spent in its transformation into a positive image each ambrotype, like each daguerreotype, is unique—one photograph only came from each exposure.

Ambrotypes do not have the mirror like appearance of daguerreotypes nor the slightly flat look of ferrotypes. They are mostly unsigned and unmarked—many were taken by the commercial while-u-wait photographers—but there is plenty of interesting, fine photography to be found within the medium.

AMERICAN UNION

A thermoplastic material, composed mainly of sawdust and shellac, used in the manufacture of cases (usually moulded with elaborate designs) for daguerreotypes and ambrotypes.

Patented by Samuel Peck on 3 October 1854.

'AT HOME' PHOTOGRAPHY

A sophisticated method of portraiture in which the subject was photographed in his or her own home and surroundings rather than the impersonal atmosphere of the photographer's studio.

Introduced during the 1880s and popular into the twentieth century.

AUTOTYPE

The double transfer system of the Carbon Print process (q.v.).

BROMOIL PRINT PROCESS

A controlled printing process in extension of the Oil Print process (q.v.), with the advantage of being suitable for enlargements as well as contact prints.

Introduced by E. J. Wall and C. Welborne Piper in 1907.

A finished print on gelatin–bromide paper was treated with a solution to bleach the black silver image and bichromate the gelatin. This was then washed in water to bring the original print to a gelatin relief image which accepted or repelled greasy inks in the same way as the ordinary oil print.

CABINET PORTRAIT

A larger version of the Carte-de-Visite photograph (q.v.).

Introduced during the very late 1860s.

Usually measuring approximately $6\frac{1}{2}$ in. by 4 in., cabinet portraits were produced by similar methods and similar photographers as the carte-de-visite photographs throughout the end of the nineteenth century and early years of the twentieth century.

Quantity rather than quality is the truth—they are still to be found in portrait albums in very large numbers—but there are some good and interesting photographs amongst the mediocre.

CALOTYPE or TALBOTYPE

The first practicable negative and positive photographic process on paper. The improved method of Photogenic Drawing (q.v.). From 'kalos' the Greek for beautiful.

Patented by William Henry Fox Talbot on 8 February 1841, in England, later the same year in France, and in 1847 in America.

Writing paper was treated with solutions of silver nitrate and potassium iodide and then dried. Just before use this was further sensitized with gallo nitrate of silver. After exposure (generally 2 or 3 minutes) the latent negative image was developed with a second solution of gallo nitrate of silver, washed and finally fixed with sodium thiosulphate (hypo).

Contact prints were then made on similarly sensitized paper under ordinary daylight. Reddish brown in colour, calotype prints are also distinguishable by their softness and completely matt surface.

The most successful exponents of the process included Talbot himself, assisted by Nicolaas Henneman, Hill and Adamson in Scotland, Hippolyte Bayard and Maxime Du Camp in France, and W. and F. Langenheim in America.

The announcement of the Wet Plate process in 1851 led Talbot to relax his patent and, within a few years, the calotype had given way entirely to the wet plate.

CAMERA OBSCURA

Literally a 'dark room'.

The phenomenon whereby a small hole in the wall of a blacked out room or box will transmit the view outside to the opposite interior wall.

Appreciated by intelligent man for at least 2,000 years.

In 1558 the Neapolitan Giovanni Battista della Porta published a detailed description of a camera obscura, advocating its use as an aid to drawing. During the seventeenth century lenses were added to sharpen and improve the scope of the images, as well as mirrors to reflect the images into more suitable positions for drawing from. Portable cameras were widely made and by the beginning of the eighteenth century they came in all shapes, sizes and disguises—imitation books, walking stick handles, a sedan chair, a coach and four—but it was the small, compact wooden cameras of the early nineteenth century that were used by Niépce, Daguerre and Talbot in their attempts and experiments to fix the image.

CARBON PRINT PROCESS

A positive printing process which gave near permanency to the finished print.

Introduced by Alphonse Louis Poitevin in 1855 and perfected by Sir Joseph Wilson Swan in 1864.

Paper was coated with bichromated gelatin (which hardens on exposure to light) containing powdered carbon, or similar pigment. During printing the exposed areas of gelatin hardened and when the print was developed and washed in water the unhardened areas of gelatin with carbon were removed to leave a positive carbon image on a fine film of insoluble gelatin. This was then transferred by a floating technique to a further sheet of paper and rinsed in an alum solution to finally harden the gelatin.

Where the image had undergone one transfer only the print was laterally reversed as in a mirror reflection, and this then required a further transfer, with an intermediary support, to right the wrong—the Double Transfer system or Autotype process.

CARTE-DE-VISITE

A small portrait photograph (although these were also topographical and other subjects) popularized by André Disdéri in the mid 1850s. Originally conceived as a supplement to the ordinary visiting card.

Usually measuring approximately $3\frac{1}{2}$ in. by $2\frac{1}{4}$ in., they were mounted on slightly larger card generally bearing the photographer's name and address and perhaps some elaborate emblem or decoration on the back.

Photographic plates and cameras were adapted to enable several exposures to be taken on a single plate—resulting in a sheet of photographs similar to a sheet of stamps.

During the 1860s hundreds of millions were sold. There were over 200 studios specializing in their production in London alone; whilst capital cities and provincial towns throughout Europe and America boasted many such establishments. Several leading artist photographers also had commercial studios engaged in their production.

Cartes-de-visite were mostly collected into specially constructed albums where the famous and admired (in England photographs of celebrities were sold for 1s. or 1s. 6d. according to demand) might rub shoulders with family friends, babies and aunties. Their popularity continued through the century although it became rather less, rather overshadowed, with the introduction of the larger Cabinet Portrait photograph (q.v.) at the very end of the 1860s.

Quantity more than quality marks the carte-de-visite. But the quality is there, and there are some wonderful and important examples of early photography within the format.

COLLOTYPE

An early photo-mechanical printing process.

Introduced by Alphonse Louis Poitevin in 1855.

A glass plate was coated with bichromated gelatin (which hardens on exposure to light). This was then gently heated and, in drying, the gelatin formed a fine reticulation grain. Following exposure under a negative and a

47

second general exposure through the back of the glass, the bichromate was washed off and the image treated with glycerine, making the less hardened areas of the surface absorbent so that the plate would accept or repell printing ink in degrees proportionate to the hardening of gelatin. Numbers of prints were then made.

COLOUR

From the very start of photography there was some disappointment that 'black and white' was the only end result—a point illustrated by the early hand tinting of daguerreotypes and ambrotypes—and yet it was well into the twentieth century before general colour photography became a reality.

Throughout the second half of the nineteenth century there raged a continual running skirmish with the problems of capturing colour.

In 1861, in London, Sir James Clerk Maxwell demonstrated the first successful attempts at colour photography. The image of a tartan ribbon being achieved by projecting one above the other, 3 matching lantern slides made through 3 different colour filters (red, green and blue) to give a single, 3-colour representation—the Additive System.

In 1869, in France, Louis Ducos du Hauron published the Subtractive System, based on the fact that pigments take away, absorb, from light all colours other than their own, which they reflect. Taking 3 separation negatives through green, orange and violet filters he then made positive carbon prints, pigmented red, blue and yellow (the complementaries of the negative colours), which were finally superimposed to make one colour picture—a Heliochrome.

These developments, far in advance of the normal technical capabilities of the day, were further limited by the lack of total sensitivity of the chemicals to all colours. Dyes were added and improvements made but it was not until the first decade of the twentieth century

that a suitable plate, the panchromatic (sensitive to all colours of the spectrum) evolved.

Meanwhile in 1891, in Philadelphia, America, Frederic Eugene Ives produced his Photochromoscope camera, an apparatus capable of taking 3 separation negatives in quick succession through red, green and blue filters. From these transparent positives were then made and viewed, superimposed, in his Kromskop, giving a single 3-colour representation in a manner similar to that devised by Sir James Clerk Maxwell.

Also in 1891, in France, Gabriel Lippmann developed his Interference System which involved the phenomenon of colours present in an apparently clear substance, like oil on water or mother of pearl. A sensitized photographic plate was placed against a layer of mercury; on exposure the mercury reflected, interfered with and divided the light into the spectrum colours. A direct positive was achieved but one which was difficult to see and impossible to reproduce, though intrinsically perfect.

Again in France, in 1904, Auguste and Louis Lumière patented the first successful Colour Screen process, an additive system, which was introduced commercially as the Autochrome in 1907. A glass plate was coated with grains of starch, dyed red, green and blue, below a layer of panchromatic emulsion. The exposure was made through the glass plate and the starch which acted as a filter. This was then developed and then re-exposed to light and re-developed (Reversal process) finally giving a colour transparency with the screen of dyed starch providing the colour.

As with all additive systems, the exposures for the autochrome were necessarily extremely long and although there were several improvements during the early twentieth century it was the subtractive system that held the qualities most suitable for modern colour photography and which formed the bases of the Kodachrome and Agfacolour films when they were eventually introduced to the public in 1935 and 1936.

COPY PHOTOGRAPHY

The merits of photography as a medium for art reproduction, copies of paintings and prints, indeed all works of art, were readily apparent from the very earliest days of its discovery.

William Henry Fox Talbot himself was, once more, one of the first to show the way; supplying over 60 calotype copy photographs to *The Annals of the Artists of Spain,* published in 1847. Several leading photographers took his example during the following decades—among them the Bisson frères, Adolphe Braun, Robert Bingham, William Lake Price and Thurston Thompson—meeting the demand for accurate copies of old master paintings as well as the popular pictures of the day.

Early copy photographs still exist in very large numbers, often in albums alongside topographical photographs. With the superiority of the modern copy processes their popularity has inevitably evaporated. Nevertheless they form an important facet of early photography, they were much desired in their time, and as such still hold an academic interest.

CYANOTYPE or BLUEPRINT PROCESS

A printing process on paper invented by Sir John Herschel in 1842.

Paper sensitized with ferric salt was exposed under the negative causing reduction of the ferric salt to ferrous and producing Turnbull's Blue, this is insoluble in water and the image was therefore fixed by washing away with water those areas unaffected by the light.

Little used photographically before the 1880s. But extensively employed into the twentieth century as a method of copying architectural and mechanical drawings.

DAGUERREOTYPE

The first ever practicable photographic process.

Given 'free to the world' by the French government on 19 August 1839 (although a patent had been taken out to cover England only 5 days before) and in wide use until the 1850s.

Invented by Louis Jacques Mandé Daguerre following his experiments in partnership with Nicéphore and Isidore Niépce.

A polished silvered copper plate was sensitized with iodine and/or bromine vapour. After exposure in the camera the positive latent image was developed with mercury vapour (a fact that Daguerre is said to have discovered quite by chance) and finally fixed with sodium thiosulphate (hypo) before sealing behind glass and framing.

The image was a direct positive with no negative which meant that there was always one only of each photograph. The detail was invariably extremely fine.

The original process, requiring an exposure of 15 to 20 minutes, was speeded up by several hands—in 1840 by J. F. Goddard, for Richard Beard, and in 1841 by Antoine Claudet and then Josef Petzval, who calculated a fast, large aperture lens for incorporation in Voigtländer cameras.

Among the most successful exponents of the process were Platt D. Babbitt, Richard Beard, Mathew B. Brady, Antoine Claudet, Alexander Ellis, J. P. Girault de Prangey, W. E. Kilburn, J. J. E. Mayall and Samuel Morse.

Daguerreotypes still exist in large numbers, often in their original cases, stamped with the photographer's name and address or sometimes moulded in American Union. They are not to be confused with Ambrotypes or Ferrotypes neither of which have the mirror like appearance of daguerreotypes—a feature which also necessitates their being viewed from a slight angle.

DRY PLATE or GELATIN EMULSION PROCESS

A negative photographic process in which the sensitizing chemicals were coated on the glass plate in a gelatin emulsion instead of wet collodion.

Following experiments by Dr. Richard Leach Maddox in 1871, the fast gelatin silver bromide plate was developed by Charles Bennett, John Burgess and Richard Kennett. In 1873 Burgess made the first gelatin dry plates for sale on the open market.

Whereas wet collodion plates had to be used immediately following sensitization, the dry plates, bought ready prepared, could be kept for long periods before use.

Prints were generally made on albumen paper until the 1890s when gelatin silver chloride or bromide paper became available.

By the early 1880s the dry plate had taken over completely from the Wet Plate. And by the late 1880s gelatin emulsion could be coated on celluloid roll film—the beginning of modern, all in, photography.

FERROTYPE or TINTYPE

A small direct positive on a black or dark brown enamelled metal plate.

Introduced by A. A. Martin in 1852/3.

The popular form of very cheap, while-u-wait, portrait photography in America, especially, and Europe during the second half of the nineteenth century and into the early twentieth century.

A thin metal plate, enamelled black or dark brown, was coated with sensitized emulsion. After exposure at as high a speed as possible, the plate dropped straight into a developer and was fixed, framed and sold often whilst still drying.

Known as American Gem Photographs when in very miniature form, ferrotypes were also mounted on card of carte-de-visite format and in jewellery, brooches, rings, cuff links and the like.

Being a direct positive the image was laterally reversed, like a mirror reflection, unless a reversing mirror had been used—this was seldom so. Also, like the daguerreotype, there was no negative and therefore one picture only came from each exposure.

Ferrotypes still exist in large numbers, in cheap golden frames or, less frequently, in jewellery and portrait albums.

GUM PRINT or GUM BICHROMATE PROCESS

A controlled printing process in which the image was formed by hardened gum containing colour pigment.

Employed from *circa* 1895, although developed during the late 1850s.

Potassium bichromate with gum arabic (which hardens on exposure to light) containing the chosen colour pigment were coated on paper. When dry this was exposed under the negative and then immersed in water to wash away the areas of gum and pigment unaffected by light and leave a finished image formed by pigment in the hardened gum.

The different colours available and manipulations possible gave great scope to the photographer and led to all sorts of variations.

HELIOGRAPH

The process devised by Nicéphore Niépce in taking the first ever photographs during the 1820s.

A glass or polished metal (pewter, zinc or silvered copper) plate was coated with bitumen of Judea (which hardens on exposure to light) and oil of lavender. After a very long exposure—up to 8 hours—the unhardened areas of bitumen were washed off by a solvent of oil of lavender and petroleum to leave a positive image formed by the varying degrees of hardened bitumen and the exposed plate.

Niépce had intended to use the plates for etching and printing from in the conventional way and several old engravings were copied for this purpose—by superimposition on the plate and exposure to light.

LANTERN SLIDES

The earliest photographic lantern slides were probably the Hyalotypes introduced in Philadelphia by W. and F. Langenheim in 1849. Diapositives on glass, they were made by the Albumen on Glass process published by Abel Niépce de St. Victor a year before.

The developments of photography and photographic lantern slides kept close in step, and by the end of the nineteenth century some exceptionally fine photographs were being made for display through the magic lantern—especially by Frederick Evans.

Sizes were standardized—$3\frac{1}{2}$ in. by 4 in. in America and Europe and $3\frac{1}{4}$ in. square in England.

MICROPHOTOGRAPH

A very much reduced photograph, generally on transparent paper or as an actual transparency. Frequently included in small souvenirs.

Not to be confused with a Photomicrograph or an American Gem photograph.

OIL PRINT PROCESS

A controlled printing process whereby oil pigment was brushed on to a gelatin relief image.

Introduced by G. E. H. Rawlins in 1904.

Paper was coated with bichromated gelatin (which hardens on exposure to light) and exposed under the negative. This was then immersed in water which the gelatin absorbed in degrees inversely proportionate to the amount affected by light, expanding and giving a relief image which accepted or repelled oil pigment, applied by brush, proportionate again to the degree of hardening or otherwise occasioned by exposure.

OXYMEL or SYRUPED COLLODION PROCESS

A negative photographic process in extension of the Wet Collodion process (q.v.).

Introduced by John Dillwyn Llewelyn in 1856.

Wet collodion plates were treated with a solution, a syrup, of vinegar and honey, enabling them to be kept for longer periods before and during use.

OZOBROME PROCESS

A controlled printing process in which an ordinary Silver Bromide Print (q.v.) was changed into a Carbon Print (q.v.).

Introduced by Thomas Manly in 1905.

Carbon tissue was treated with a solution which sensitized it and impregnated it with potassium ferricyanide and potassium bromide. This was then pressed into contact with a silver bromide print for about half an hour so that the pigmented gelatin hardened wherever it had been against the silver image of the original print. The carbon tissue was then separated and developed in the normal way.

OZOTYPE

A controlled printing process in extension of the Carbon Print (q.v.), with the advantage that there was no transfer of the image and therefore no lateral reversion.

Introduced by Thomas Manly in 1899.

Paper was coated with bichromated gelatin containing manganous salts and exposed under the negative to give a faint image. This was then pressed into contact with a sheet of tissue which had been coated with gelatin containing the chosen colour pigment and immersed in an acid solution. The acid acted on the original image so that it slowly penetrated and hardened the overlying areas of pigmented gelatin. The tissue was then removed and then development followed in the same way as the carbon print.

PHOTOGENIC DRAWING

The earliest negative and positive photographic process on paper.

Invented by William Henry Fox Talbot, *circa* 1835. Published in January 1839 when Talbot began to hear of Daguerre's progress.

Writing paper was sensitized with silver chloride and silver nitrate and exposed in a camera, for a very long while. The resultant negative image was fixed with a common salt solution. Printing being achieved by contact with similarly sensitized paper.

In September 1840 Talbot discovered the existence of a latent image, present after only a short exposure, that could be developed with gallo nitrate of silver. The improved, now practicable, method became the Calotype process (q.v.).

PHOTOGRAVURE

A photo-mechanical printing process in which the image was reproduced from a photo-engraved, photo-etched, metal plate.

Developed by Karl Klic, *circa* 1879. Later, *circa* 1895, improved into the Rotogravure process in which engraved cylinders replaced the plates.

A polished metal (usually copper) plate was coated with dust of resin or bitumen, which adhered with mild heating, to form a grain. A carbon print (q.v.) was then made from a diapositive (a transparency) giving a negative image which was transferred to the grained copper plate. Next this was washed in warm water, to remove the soluble parts of the carbon image, and the plate etched—usually with a solution of ferric chloride. After clearing off the gelatin, which had formed the body of the carbon print, the plate was seen to be etched in varying depths proportionate to the tones of the original picture; the shadows being the deepest and so holding the most ink when printing began.

PHOTOMICROGRAPH

A photograph taken through a microscope.

Not to be confused with a Microphotograph.

Between 1839 and 1841 both L. J. M. Daguerre and William Henry Fox Talbot made photomicrographs via their respective photographic inventions. Talbot's calotypes of butterfly wings and botanical sections are among the most remarkable and rare items of all early photography.

PLATINOTYPE

A high quality printing process in which platinum was used in place of silver salts, with the advantages of permanence and the finest tones.

Patented by William Willis in 1873.

Paper coated with platinum chloride and ferric oxalate was exposed under the negative and then developed by washing with potassium oxalate, leaving a pure platinum image. This could be toned if desired.

The superior qualities of the platinotype were held in such esteem by artist photographers that several gave up photography completely when platinum became so scarce and expensive during the First World War as to force the demise of the process.

POSTCARDS

The first postcards were introduced in 1869, in Austria; the first picture postcards during the late 1880s.

Between the mid 1890s and *circa* 1914 picture postcards enjoyed their widest use and greatest popularity. Many were straightforward photographs, readily distinguishable, simply altered in format to fit the official postcard size.

Attributing photographic postcards to specific photographers may be impossible. Most are unmarked (although those by Francis Frith & Co. are one of several notable exceptions) and many were made up to private order, as records of some special occasion or view, from the lesser known commercial and provincial photographers.

SILVER BROMIDE PRINT

The most widely used modern type of paper print.

Introduced *circa* 1880.

Paper was coated and sensitized with a gelatin emulsion containing silver bromide and a small amount of silver iodide.

SOCIETIES AND GROUPS

The first photographic societies started to appear in France and England during the late 1840s and early 1850s.

The Calotype Club was formed in 1847, the Société Héliographique in 1851, the Photographic Society of London in 1853 and the Société Française de Photographie in 1854.

The Photographic Society of London, created by Roger Fenton, is now the oldest society of its kind in the world, holding regular exhibitions and still publishing *The Photographic Journal*—a magazine first produced in March 1853. The society became the Photographic Society of Great Britain in 1874 and the Royal Photographic Society of Great Britain twenty years later.

The Société Française de Photographie likewise is still extremely active, in Paris, holding exhibitions of photographs with similar regularity.

Other groups and societies came along during the latter half of the nineteenth century and early years of the twentieth century; among them The International Society of Pictorial Photographers (founded in 1904 with James Craig Annan as the first president and the aims of unifying and furthering art photography in all nations) and, most important of all, the Linked Ring Brotherhood and Photo-Secession.

The Linked Ring Brotherhood of artist photographers was formed in 1892 as a breakaway group from the Photographic Society of Great Britain, chiefly in protest at the society's lack of welcome for naturalistic and impressionistic art photography. Founder members included Alfred Horsley Hinton (at the head), George Davison, Henry Peach Robinson and Frank Meadows Sutcliffe. They were joined by most of the leading artist photographers in Europe and America except, surprisingly, Peter Henry Emerson. Annual exhibitions were held at the London Salon up to 1914.

Photo-Secession was founded by Alfred Stieglitz in New York in 1902, with similar ideals as the Linked Ring and in disatisfaction with the standards and outlook of the photographic establishment. Several members of the Linked Ring Brotherhood were members of Photo-Secession as well. In 1905 Stieglitz, with Edward Steichen, opened the Photo-Secession gallery at 291 Fifth Avenue, New York, where paintings and sculpture as well as photographs were shown in regular exhibitions. The gallery later came to be known simply as the '291'.

The Linked Ring Brotherhood and Photo-Secession were the two most significant and influential movements, groups, in early creative photography.

STEREOSCOPE

A binocular device for viewing in three dimensions.

Developed by Sir Charles Wheatstone in 1838, for geometric designs, the stereoscope advanced with photography from 1845 and became widely popular after the Great Exhibition of 1851.

Two almost identical photographs, taken from just slightly different points, were mounted side by side and when viewed through the apparatus they merged to form a single, 3-dimensional, representation.

Stereoscope photographs could be taken with one exposure through a special double lens camera; or with two, through an ordinary camera, minutely altering the angle for the second exposure.

Popular throughout the second half of the nineteenth century and into the early twentieth century, the apparatus brought new as well as established photographers and types of photography within its compass.

Daguerreotype stereoscope slides, some with attached viewing screens, were frequently produced but most slides were made from wet or dry plate photographs and are topographical in subject matter. Francis Bedford, George Washington Wilson and others made series of topographical photographs specially for the stereoscope, whilst the London Stereoscopic & Photographic Company published many thousands of views during the 1850s and 60s, and at the end of the century Underwood & Underwood were handling collections and series in very large numbers.

TANNIN PROCESS

A negative photographic process in extension of the Wet Plate process (q.v.).

Introduced by Charles Russell in 1861.

Wet collodion plates were treated with tannin as a preservative, enabling them to be kept for longer periods after sensitization and so allow longer exposures—particularly required for some interior work.

WAXED PAPER PROCESS

A variant on the Calotype (q.v.) in which the negative was made on paper permeated with wax to give greater transparency and greater definition in the final print. In addition, the waxed and sensitized paper could be kept for some 10 to 14 days before use—against one day for ordinary calotype paper.

Introduced by Gustave Le Gray in 1851.

WET PLATE or WET COLLODION PROCESS

A negative photographic process in which wet collodion held the sensitizing chemicals on a glass plate.

Invented by Frederick Scott Archer in 1851.

Collodion (a viscous transparent substance) with potassium iodide was poured over a glass plate. This was immediately sensitized with silver nitrate and exposed in the camera while still wet, as the chemicals deteriorated if the collodion was allowed to dry. The latent negative image was developed, also immediately, with pyrogallic acid or ferrous sulphate and then fixed with sodium thiosulphate (hypo).

The glass negative could be used to make ordinary prints (generally on albumen paper) or, by treatment, be transformed into 'positive' images—Ambrotypes (q.v.).

Free of any patent, the wet plate heralded the general expansion of photography. In addition it was the fastest process of its time, with exposures as short as 10 seconds and even less when adapted for 'instantaneous' exposures in stereoscopic cameras and other devices. But, there was one major disadvantage—the need to sensitize, expose and develop the plates all within a very short time—a great hindrance to any mobile or itinerant photographer who was obliged to transport all the cumbersome equipment wherever he ventured.

In general widespread use from its introduction until the arrival of the Dry Plate process (q.v.) in the 1870s.

WOODBURYTYPE

An early mass printing process in which photographic prints could be continuously reproduced.

Introduced by Walter Bentley Woodbury in 1864/5.

A relief image in gelatin was made, following printing from the negative, in a manner similar to the Oil Print process (q.v.). This was then laid and pressed on a lead plate to transfer and transform the image into an intaglio. Prints were finally pulled from the lead plate in the way of ordinary printing.

Mainly used in book illustration, during the second half of the nineteenth century, woodburytypes are identifiable by their lack of any grain or dot formation and their slightly purple colour.

The Modern Market and Early Photographs—Some Prices Recorded

The commercial interchange of early photographs is a very new facet of the wide art world. This is strange, for the discovery of photography in the early nineteenth century was certainly one of the major events in the history of mankind, let alone the history of the nineteenth century; and it is the nineteenth century and the art and artefacts of the nineteenth century that have been the subject of such intensive attention and commercial interest during the last decade or so—with the exception of photography.

The prejudice against photography as an art dies very hard—'Oh! but it's only a photograph!' is the familiar and foolish cry. A senseless statement.

Still, there is a silver lining, for as long as the prejudice continues it constitutes a welcome, if paradoxical, ally for the buyers of early photographs. Very few of the smarter art and antique shops would dream, at the moment, of including photographs in their stock. Photographs in most eyes are for the jumble and rummage sales, the junk shops, and this is where many are to be found, where they may cost just a few pence, occasionally a pound or two, and sometimes are even given away. Much, indeed, is worth only a few pence, or deserves no more than to be given away: one has to search for the quality in all the quantity, for the cream. The cream that is now starting to appear at the other end of the scale, in the awesome auction rooms, where £410 is given for a single print of William Henry Fox Talbot's 'Chess Players', £4,800 for an album of calotypes by David Octavius Hill and Robert Adamson, and £270 for Julia Margaret Cameron's portrait of Sir John Herschel.

There follows a brief list of commercial events in the embryo market for early photographs in England. Obviously only a small proportion, a mere fraction, of the different types of photograph and work of different photographers has so far come on to the market to establish a permanent price pattern, but it is hoped that from the facts—all the figures given are based on actual auction prices recorded—the curious reader will be able to calculate the foundations of a price guide. Yet, caution, caution. Time flies fast in the commercial world and the price of a photograph on one given day may be completely different a month or two later. Whilst the existence or not of negatives, the numbers of any one print originally made by the photographer, and the likelihood of quantities (or none) of the same print turning up again, are thoughts and possibilities to be kept continually in mind.

55

Ambrotypes

Single small and ordinary portraits, attributed or unattributed £1 to £15 each
Single more interesting portraits, attributed or unattributed £15 to £70 each
Single subject photographs, unattributed £48 and £58 each

    (The low figure for a ¼ plate ambrotype of Niagara Falls; the high one for a whole plate of a heraldic artist outside his studio.)

See also—J. J. E. Mayall.

Books

Ruined Abbeys and Castles of Great Britain and Ireland by William and Mary Howitt, with 27 photographs by Francis Bedford, Roger Fenton, Russell Sedgefield and others, 1862 edition only £42

The Lord of the Isles by Sir Walter Scott, with 9 photographs by S. Thompson and Russell Sedgefield, 1871 edition £12

See also—William Barraud
        Julia Margaret Cameron
        Alvin Langdon Coburn
        Charles Piazzi Smyth
        William Henry Fox Talbot
        John Thomson.

Calotypes

Single calotypes, topographical and general subjects, unattributed £4 to £20 each
Single calotypes, portraits, group portraits and subject photographs, attributed £18 to £560 each

See also—David Octavius Hill and Robert Adamson
        William Henry Fox Talbot.

Carte-de-Visite and Cabinet Portrait Photographs

Single ordinary portraits by lesser known photographers 5p to 50p each
Single portraits of well known figures, writers, artists, statesmen and royalty, by the better known photographers 10p to £3 each
Single subject photographs 20p to £2 each

Daguerreotypes

Single portraits, unattributed £5 to £40 each
Single portraits, attributed £8 to £50 each

See also—Richard Beard
    William Constable
    W. E. Kilburn
    R. Lowe
    J. J. E. Mayall
    S. L. Walker

Single subject photographs, attributed   £70 to £225 each
See also—Platt D. Babbitt
    M. de St. Croix

Single daguerreotype stereoscope slides, portraits and subject
photographs, attributed and unattributed   £30 to £130 each
 (The high figure for a rare slide of the interior of the Crystal
 Palace, with Napoleon III and Queen Victoria, taken on
 20 April 1855.)
See also—Antoine Claudet
    J. J. E. Mayall

Ferrotypes

Single small and ordinary portraits, attributed or unattributed 50p to £5 each

Stereoscope Slides

Single stereoscope slides from photographs on paper mounted
on card   20p to £8 each
 (The low figure for slides of small topographical interest;
 the high one for a rare slide by Francis Frith of the photographer's headquarters in an apparently Near Eastern landscape,
 signed in the plate.)

Single daguerreotype stereoscope slides, portraits and subject
photographs, attributed and unattributed   £30 to £130 each
 (The high figure for a rare slide of the interior of the Crystal
 Palace, with Napoleon III and Queen Victoria, taken on
 20 April 1855.)
See also—Antoine Claudet
    J. J. E. Mayall

Portrait Albums

Family albums of carte-de-visite and cabinet portrait photographs, mixed sitters and photographers   £2 to £30 per album
See also—Carte-de-Visite and Cabinet Portrait Photographs.

Topographical and General Albums

Albums of mixed topographical and general photographs of the second half of the nineteenth century, unattributed or by lesser known photographers £5 to £20 per album

Similar albums, but including unusual photographs and/or examples by well known photographers £5 to £95 per album
  (The number of good photographs, involving figures as well as topography and landscape, controls the price. As a rule, £2 to £8 per good photograph has added up to give the final result.)

See also—Francis Bedford
        Samuel Bourne
        J. David

Special albums, by the most prominent of nineteenth century photographers or on rare subjects £137 to £4,800 per album

See also—Julia Margaret Cameron
        David Octavius Hill and Robert Adamson

Platt D. Babbitt

Single daguerreotypes, subject photographs—the Niagara Falls £70 to £80 each

William Barraud

Book—*Men and Women of the Day, A Picture Gallery of Contemporary Portraiture*, 2 volumes, 1888 and 1889 £79 the two

Richard Beard

Single daguerreotype portraits, in marked cases £18 to £40 each

Francis Bedford

Album—An album of 10 'Photographic Views of Exeter' £21

Samuel Bourne

Album—An album of 82 photographs of India, Indian and Himalayan subjects, *circa* 1873 £50

58

Julia Margaret Cameron

Single portrait photographs £30 to £270 each
(The high figure for a portrait of Sir John Herschel, fully
signed by Mrs. Cameron and the sitter.)

Single and subject photographs £9 to £126 each
(The low figure for a poor print of 'The Lily and the Lamb';
the high one for 'The Kiss of Peace', fully signed, dated and
inscribed.)

Books and albums £137 to £420 per
(The low figure for an album of 19 small, 6 in. by 4 in., sub- volume
ject photographs; the high one for Volume 1 of *Illustrations
to Tennyson's Idylls of the King and Other Poems*, 13 photographs each inscribed and signed.)

The present condition of Mrs. Cameron's photographs varies
very widely, and the lower prices recorded are for badly torn
or faded examples.

Lewis Carroll

Single portrait of Tennyson, 9½ in. by 7¼ in. £231

Antoine Claudet

Single daguerreotype stereoscope slides, portraits £65 to £85 each

Alvin Langdon Coburn

Single landscape and topographical photographs, controlled
process prints from the early 1900s £19 to £62 each
(The low figure for a London view, 5¾ in. by 3½ in.; the high
one for a Thames view, 8½ in. by 6¾ in. Both prints were
signed and inscribed.)

Books—*London*, with 20 photogravures, 1909 £85
London by G. K. Chesterton, with 10 photogravures,
1914 £52

William Constable

Single dageurreotype portraits £18 to £42 each
(The high figure for a portrait of a girl, signed with initials
and dated 1847.)

Edward S. Curtis

Single photogravures of North American Indians, portraits and figure subjects, large format (approximately 18 in. by 12 in.)   £10 to £19 each

J. David

Album—An album of 52 photographs of the Royal Military College, Sandhurst, 1886   £42

J. J. Eastmead

Single photograph of the sale of Dickens's furniture, 'The Last Lot', June 1870, labelled   £10

Francis Frith

Single topographical photographs, by Francis Frith or his assistants   £1 to £30 each
   (The high figure for 'The Mosque of Qaitbey, Cairo', 15 in. by 18 in., signed and dated 1858 in the plate.)

Single stereoscope slides   50p to £8 each
   (The high figure for a rare paper photograph on card of the photographer's headquarters in an apparently Near Eastern landscape, signed in the plate.)

Groom & Company

Single marine photographs   £4 to £8 each

James Hedderley

Single topographical photograph of Chelsea Reach, 11 in. by 14 in., labelled   £34

David Octavius Hill and Robert Adamson

Single calotypes, portraits, group portraits and subject photographs   £18 to £560 each
   (The low figure for a faded portrait of a little known sitter; the high one for a fine photograph, in good condition, of a Newhaven fisherman.)

Album—An album of 32 calotype photographs of well known subjects and portraits   £4,800

W. E. Kilburn

Single daguerreotype portraits, in marked cases   £16 to £31 each

R. Lowe

Single daguerreotype portraits, in marked cases   £17 and £18 each

J. J. E. Mayall

Single daguerreotype portraits, in marked cases   £40 to £45 each

Single daguerreotype stereoscope slides, portraits   £80 to £90 each

Single ambrotype small portrait   £8

C. Naya

Single topographical photographs of Venice   £1 to £2 each

Charles Piazzi Smyth

Book—*Teneriffe: An Astronomer's Experiment, or Specialities of a Residence above the Clouds*, with 20 stereoscopic photographs, 1858   £38 and £40 each

Giorgio Sommer

Single photographs of Neapolitan figure subjects   £1 each

M. de St. Croix

Single daguerreotypes, topographical photographs of Paris and London, taken in 1839, believed to be by de St. Croix   £150 to £225 each

Frank Meadows Sutcliffe

Single photographs, genre and landscape subjects   £1 to £115 each
    (The low figure for an unmarked topographical photograph of small interest and size; the high one for a print of 'Whitby Harbour in a Mist', 8 in. by $11\frac{1}{2}$ in., signed on the surface.)

William Henry Fox Talbot

Single calotypes, topographical and subject photographs   £125 to £410 each
(The low figure for an 'Italian View'; the high one for the 'Chess Players'.)

Single calotype negatives   £60 to £150 each
(The low figure for an 'Avenue of Trees'; the high one for 'Cottages'.)

Books—*The Pencil of Nature*, missing 3 of the 24 photographs but sold with 1 extra   £2,500

Sun Pictures in Scotland, with 23 photographs   £1,000 and £1,300 each

John Thomson

Book—*Street Life in London*, a volume illustrated by 36 wood-burytypes (missing the text)   £231

James Valentine

Single topographical photographs, by James Valentine or his assistants   £1 to £6 each

S. L. Walker

Single daguerreotype portraits, in marked cases   £8 to £20 each

George Washington Wilson

Single topographical photographs, by George Washington Wilson or his assistants   £1 to £5 each

62

Bibliography

The History of Photography by Helmut and Alison Gernsheim, revised edition, Thames & Hudson, London, 1969.

The History of Photography, 1839 to the Present Day by Beaumont Newhall, Museum of Modern Art, New York, 1949.

The Picture History of Photography by Peter Pollack, revised edition, Harry N. Abrams, New York, 1969.

The First Negatives by D. B. Thomas, Science Museum, London, 1964.

The Focal Encyclopedia of Photography, Focal Press, London, 1965.

Photography of Today by H. Chapman Jones, Seeley, Service & Company, London, 1913.

British Photographers by Cecil Beaton, William Collins, London, 1944.

Photography and the American Scene by Robert Taft, MacMillan, New York, 1938.

American Daguerreian Art by Floyd and Marion Rinhart, Clarkson N. Potter, New York, 1967.

America and Alfred Stieglitz: a Collective Portrait, Doubleday, Doran & Company, New York, 1934.

Photo-Secession: Photography as a Fine Art by Robert Doty, The George Eastman House, New York, 1960.

Art and Photography by Aaron Scharf, Allen Lane, London, 1968.

Julia Margaret Cameron by Helmut Gernsheim, Fountain Press, London, 1948.

Roger Fenton, Photographer of the Crimean War, Essay by Helmut and Alison Gernsheim, Secker & Warburg, London, 1954.

Lewis Carroll—Photographer by Helmut Gernsheim, revised edition, Dover, New York, 1969.

Alex. Keighley, Artist and Photographer, Royal Photographic Society, London, 1947.

David Octavius Hill and Robert Adamson, Scottish Arts Council exhibition catalogue, Edinburgh, 1970.

Masterpiece, Royal Photographic Society and Arts Council exhibition catalogue, London, 1971.

The Beginnings of Photography, 'From today painting is dead', Victoria and Albert Museum exhibition catalogue, London, 1972.

Illustrations

GERNSHEIM COLLECTION, UNIVERSITY OF TEXAS: 1 and 10.

SOCIÉTÉ FRANÇAISE DE PHOTOGRAPHIE, PARIS: 2, 3, 7, 17, 18, 30 and 179.

BIBLIOTHÈQUE NATIONALE, PARIS: 4, 22, 27, 28, 29, 32, 33, 34, 38, 39, 52, 53, 54, 74, 75, 150, 151, 152, 177, 178, 180, 207, 208, 209, 210, 211 and 212.

SCIENCE MUSEUM, LONDON: 5, 6, 11, 12, 13, 14, 15, 16, 46 and 78.

VICTORIA AND ALBERT MUSEUM, LONDON: 19, 20, 21, 31, 35, 36, 37, 40, 42, 47, 48, 49, 50, 56, 57, 58, 62, 63, 65, 66, 67, 68, 69, 70, 79, 87, 88, 89, 90, 91, 92, 95, 96, 97, 98, 99, 101, 102, 103, 104, 105, 106, 109, 110, 111, 112, 116, 120, 121, 122, 123, 127, 131, 134, 135, 136, 137, 144, 145, 146, 147, 148, 149, 153, 155, 156, 174, 175, 176, 183, 184, 185, 186, 187, 188, 217, 218, 219, 220 and 223.

ROYAL PHOTOGRAPHIC SOCIETY OF GREAT BRITAIN, LONDON: 23, 24, 25, 26, 43, 44, 45, 51, 118, 119, 215, 221, 222, 224, 225, 226, 227, 228, 229, 230, 231, 232, 233, 234, 235, 236, 237, 238, 239, 240, 242, 243, 244, 245, 246, 247, 248, 249, 250, 251 and 252.

NATIONAL PORTRAIT GALLERY, LONDON: 41.

LIBRARY OF THE UNIVERSITY OF PENNSYLVANIA: 71, 72 and 73.

BIBLIOTHÈQUE DES MONUMENTS HISTORIQUES, PARIS: 114 and 115.

MORRIS L. PARRISH COLLECTION OF VICTORIAN NOVELISTS, PRINCETON UNIVERSITY LIBRARY, PRINCETON: 124, 125 and 126.

LIBRARY OF CONGRESS, WASHINGTON: 138.

BEKEN of COWES, ISLE OF WIGHT: 190.

MISS C. PATTISON: 191, 192, 193, 194, 195 and 196.

BETTMANN ARCHIVE INC., NEW YORK: 205.

INTERNATIONAL MUSEUM OF PHOTOGRAPHY, NEW YORK: 206.

MUSEUM OF MODERN ART, NEW YORK: 241.

S. & O. MATHEWS: 8, 9, 55, 59, 60, 61, 64, 76, 77, 80, 81, 82, 83, 84, 85, 86, 93, 94, 100, 107, 108, 113, 117, 128, 129, 130, 132, 133, 139, 140, 141, 142, 143, 154, 157, 158, 159, 160, 161, 162, 163, 164, 165, 166, 167, 168, 169, 170, 171, 172, 173, 181, 182, 189, 197, 198, 199, 200, 201, 202, 203, 204, 213, 214, and 216.

I

1. NICÉPHORE NIÉPCE. The earliest photograph known
to exist. An 8 hour exposure taken from an upstairs
window. Heliograph. 1826.

2. NICÉPHORE NIÉPCE. Copy of a heliograph of un-
certain date—both 1822 and 1829 have been suggested.

2

3

3. L. J. M. DAGUERRE. Still life. Daguerreotype. 1837/9.
4. J. P. GIRAULT de PRANGEY. The Tuileries Gardens.
   Daguerreotype. 1841/2.

4

5

5. and 6. ALEXANDER ELLIS. Roman architecture.
   Daguerreotypes. 1841.

6

7

7. JEAN FOUCAULT. Grapes. Daguerreotype. *c.* 1845.

8. RICHARD BEARD. Portrait. Daguerreotype. *c.* 1850.

9. W. E. KILBURN. Portrait. Tinted daguerreotype. *c.* 1850.

10. PLATT D. BABBITT. The Niagara river with a man stranded on rocks. Daguerreotype. 1854.

8

9

10

11

11. WILLIAM HENRY FOX TALBOT. Positive print from the earliest negative known to exist. Photogenic Drawing. 1835.

12. WILLIAM HENRY FOX TALBOT. Chess Players. Calotype. *c.* 1841.

13. WILLIAM HENRY FOX TALBOT. Woodcutters. Calotype. *c.* 1842.

14. WILLIAM HENRY FOX TALBOT. 4 girls. Calotype. April 1842.

12

13

14

15. WILLIAM HENRY FOX TALBOT. Nicolaas Henneman holding the title page of *The Pencil of Nature*. Calotype. 1844.

16. WILLIAM HENRY FOX TALBOT. The photographic establishment at Reading. Calotype. *c.* 1845.

15

16

17

17. HIPPOLYTE BAYARD. Still life. Calotype. *c.* 1845.
18. HIPPOLYTE BAYARD. Montmartre. Calotype. *c.*1845.

18

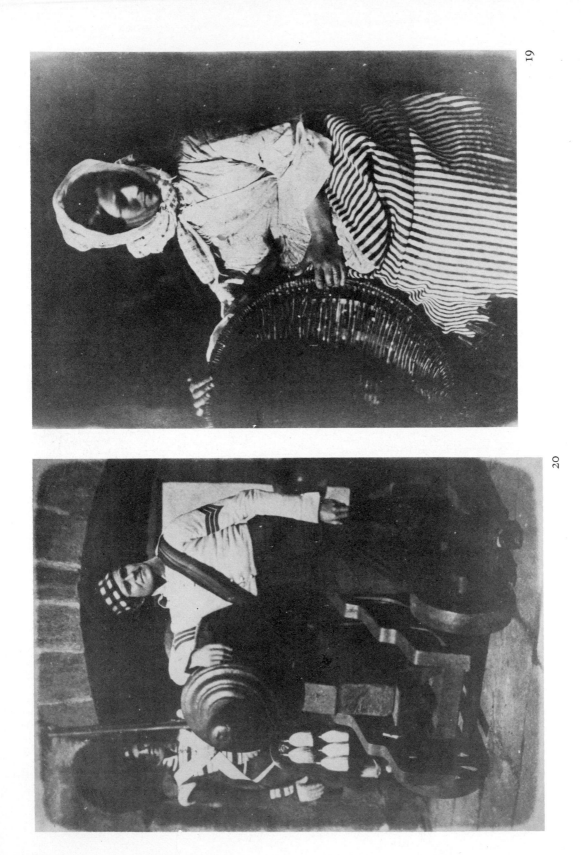

74

19. HILL and ADAMSON. Elizabeth Johnstone, The Beautiful Fishwife. Calotype. *c.* 1845.

20. HILL and ADAMSON. Gordon Highlanders at Edinburgh Castle. Calotype. April 1846.

21. HILL and ADAMSON. Newhaven seaman, Jas. Linton, and boys. Calotype. 1845.

21

22. HENRI LE SECQ. Dieppe. Calotype. *c.* 1851.

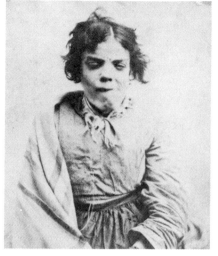

23

24

25

26

23, 24, 25 and 26. HUGH DIAMOND. Mental patients.
    c. 1850/3.

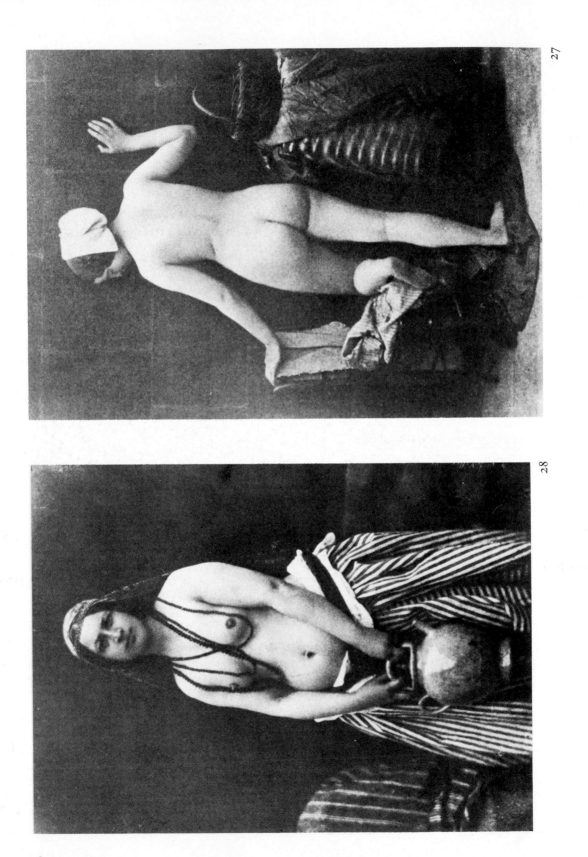

27, 28 and 29. JULIEN de VILLENEUVE. Nudes. *c.* 1850/3.

29

30

30. HENRI REGNAULT. Seated boy. Calotype. *c.* 1852.
31. MAXIME DU CAMP. The Sphinx. 1849.

31

32

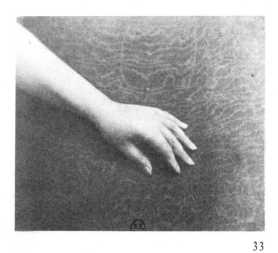

33

34

32. CHARLES VICTOR HUGO. Victor Hugo. 1853/5.
33. CHARLES VICTOR HUGO. Madame Victor Hugo's arm. 1853/5.
34. CHARLES VICTOR HUGO. Victor Hugo's cat. 1853/5.

35

35. JAMES ROBERTSON. The Tower of the Winds,
    Athens. *c.* 1853.

36. JAMES ROBERTSON. The Crimean War. An aban-
    doned battery. 1855/6.

37. ROGER FENTON. The Crimean War. Hardships in
    the Camp. 1855.

36

37

38

39

40

38. CHARLES LANGLOIS and L. MÉHÉVIN. The Crimean War. Pièce Russe. 1855/6.

39. CHARLES LANGLOIS. The Crimean War. Canrobert's redoubt at Inkerman. 1855.

40. FELICE A. BEATO. The Indian Mutiny. Lucknow. 1857.

41. ROBERT HOWLETT. Isambard Brunel. 1857.

41

42

42. CHARLES CLIFFORD. Madrid. 1853.

43. OSCAR REJLANDER. The Two Ways of Life. 1857.
    A photograph made up from over 30 different
    negatives.

44. OSCAR REJLANDER. The head of John the Baptist.
    1856.

43

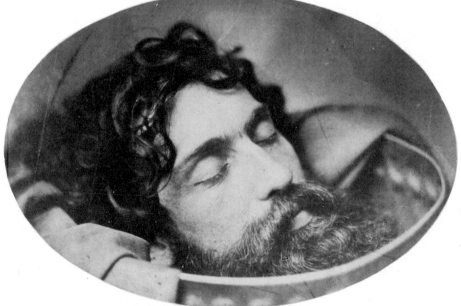

44

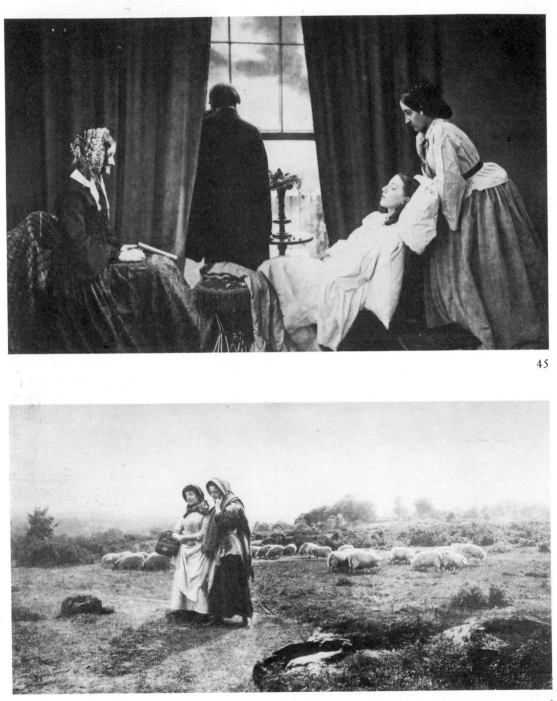

45

46

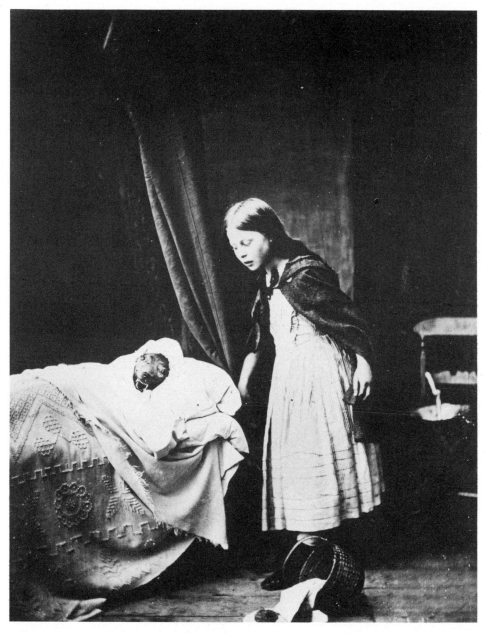

47

45. HENRY PEACH ROBINSON. Fading Away. 1858.
46. HENRY PEACH ROBINSON. Carrolling.
47. HENRY PEACH ROBINSON. Little Red Riding
    Hood. 1858/62.

C. Silvy

48. CAMILLE SILVY. River scene, France. 1858.
49. CAMILLE SILVY. Sheep. *c.* 1858/60.

50. ROGER FENTON. The Keeper's Rest, Ribbleside.
    c. 1858/60.
51. ROGER FENTON. Still life, fruit and flowers. c. 1860.

51

52

52. DÉSIRÉ CHARNAY. The Grand Palace at Mitla.
    c. 1859.
53. ADOLPHE BRAUN. Panorama of Strasbourg. 1859.
54. ADOLPHE BRAUN. Strasbourg Cathedral. 1859.

53

54

55

56

57

58

55. Carte-de-visite, Napoleon III by ANDRÉ DISDÉRI.
    c. 1854.

56. Carte-de-visite, Emile Zola by MÉLANDRI. *c.* 1870.

57. Carte-de-visite, George Sand by NADAR. 1866.

58. Carte-de-visite, Gustave Courbet by CH. REUT-
    LINGER. *c.* 1865/70.

59

60

61

62

59. Carte-de-visite, by ANDRÉ DISDÉRI. *c.* 1860.

60. Carte-de-visite, by DISDÉRI et CIE. *c.* 1858.

61. Carte-de-visite, by J. J. E. MAYALL. March 1861.

62. Carte-de-visite, Prince Albert by J. J. E. MAYALL.
   c. 1858.

63

64

65

66

63. Carte-de-visite, John Ruskin by ELLIOTT and FRY. c. 1860.

64. Carte-de-visite, Garibaldi by J. J. E. MAYALL. April 1864.

65. Carte-de-visite, Dr. Livingstone by THOMAS ANNAN. 1864.

66. Carte-de-visite, Baron Charles Marochetti by MAULL and POLYBLANK. c. 1865.

67

68

69

70

67. Carte-de-visite, John Heenan by C. D. FREDERICKS. 1862.

68. Carte-de-visite, Abraham Lincoln by EDWARD ANTHONY. 1863/4.

69. Carte-de-visite, Edward Sothern as Garrick by NAPOLEON SARONY and CO. c. 1865.

70. Carte-de-visite, General U.S. Grant by ALEXANDER GARDNER. 1865.

71

72

73

71. ALEXANDER GARDNER. The American Civil War. Home of a Rebel Sharpshooter, Gettysburg. 1863.

72. ALEXANDER GARDNER and TIMOTHY H. O'SULLIVAN. The American Civil War. The Harvest of Death, Gettysburg. 1863.

73. ALEXANDER GARDNER. The American Civil War. 'What do I want John Henry?' 1862.

74

74. NADAR. Edouard Manet. *c.* 1864.
75. NADAR. Self portrait. *c.* 1863.

75

76

76. Ambrotype. Photographer unknown. *c*. 1860.

77. A. L. HENDERSON. Bicyclist. *c*. 1865 (from a carte-de-visite).

78. J. MOFFAT. William Henry Fox Talbot. *c*. 1865 (from a carte-de-visite).

77

78

79

80

81

82

79. Carte-de-visite, by ETIENNE CARJAT. *c*. 1864.

80. Carte-de-visite, by FRANK MEADOWS SUTCLIFFE. *c*. 1875.

81. Carte-de-visite. Photographer unknown. *c*. 1865.

82. Carte-de-visite, Thomas Carlyle by THE LONDON STEREOSCOPIC and PHOTOGRAPHIC COMPANY. *c*. 1870.

83

84

85

86

83. Carte-de-visite, by OLIVIER SARONY and CO. *c.* 1880.

84. Carte-de-visite, by HENNAH and KENT. *c.* 1875.

85. Carte-de-visite, by HEATH and BEAU. *c.* 1870.

86. Carte-de-visite, by HILLS and SAUNDERS. *c.* 1880.

87

88

89

90

87. Carte-de-visite, by ABDULLAH FRÈRES. *c.* 1865.

88. Carte-de-visite, by BOURNE and SHEPHERD. *c.* 1865.

89 and 90. Cartes-de-visite, Maoris by J. CORBETT. *c.* 1865.

91

92

93

94

91. Carte-de-visite, H. J. Coxwell by NEGRETTI and ZAMBRA. 1863.

92. Carte-de-visite, H. J. Coxwell and James Glaisher by NEGRETTI and ZAMBRA. 1863.

93. Carte-de-visite. Photographer unknown. *c.* 1860.

94. Carte-de-visite, by K. TAMOTO. 1891.

95. SAMUEL BOURNE. The Kutb Minar, Delhi. *c.* 1865.
96. CARLO PONTI. Venice. *c.* 1860.

95

96

97

97. GUSTAVE LE GRAY. The Sun at Noon. *c.* 1856.
98. GUSTAVE LE GRAY. Ships in Harbour. *c.* 1860.

98

99

99. EDOUARD BALDUS. La Chapelle de St. Pont. *c.* 1865.

100. GROOM and COMPANY. The Impregnable. 1869.

101. GUSTAVE LE GRAY. The Pope's carriage. 1863.

100

101

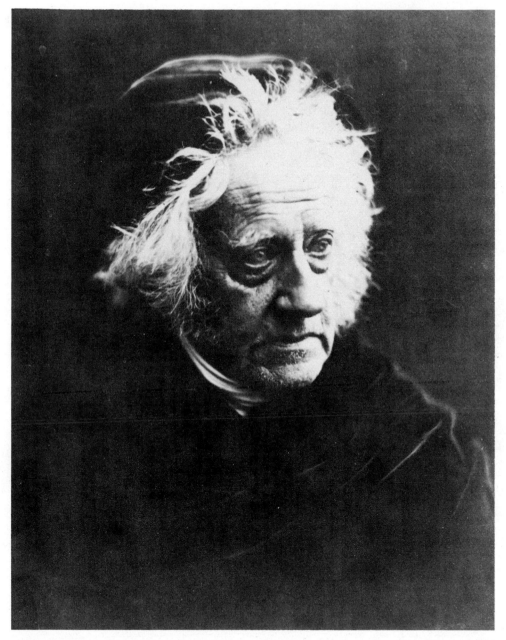

104

102. JULIA MARGARET CAMERON. Alfred Lord Tennyson. June 1869.

103. JULIA MARGARET CAMERON. Charles Darwin.
1869.

104. JULIA MARGARET CAMERON. Sir John Herschel.
1867.

105. JULIA MARGARET CAMERON. The Return after Three Days. *c,* 1868/70.

106. JULIA MARGARET CAMERON. The Angel at the Sepulchre. *c.* 1868.

107. JULIA MARGARET CAMERON. Child drawing. *c.* 1870.

107

108

108. JULIA MARGARET CAMERON. The Kiss of Peace. 1869.

109. JULIA MARGARET CAMERON. Illustration for *Lancelot and Elaine*. *c.* 1873.

110. HENRY HERSCHEL HAY CAMERON. Julia Margaret Cameron. *c.* 1875.

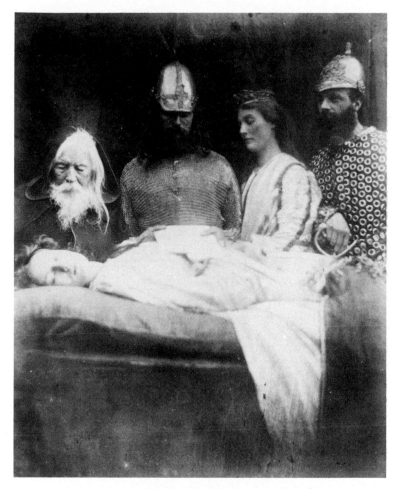

109

110

117

III

III. FRANCIS FRITH. Title page of *The Gossiping Photographer at Hastings.* 1864.

112. FRANCIS FRITH. St. Clement's Church, Hastings. 1864.

113. FRANCIS FRITH. Scarborough. *c.* 1880.

112

113

114

115

114. CHARLES MARVILLE. The erection of the column in the Place Vendôme, Paris.

115. CHARLES MARVILLE. Placing the statue of Napoleon on the column in the Place Vendôme, Paris. December 1875.

116. P. H. DELAMOTTE. Magdalen College Oxford— illustration for *The Sunbeam*. 1859.

116

117. JAMES HEDDERLY. Old Chelsea Reach. *c.* 1870.

118. JOHN THOMSON. Public Disinfectors—illustration
for *Street Life in London*. Woodburytype. 1877.

119. JOHN THOMSON. The Street Doctor—illustration
for *Street Life in London*. Woodburytype. 1877.

118

119

120

121

122

120, 121, 122 and 123. CLEMENTINA HAWARDEN.
Figure subjects. c. 1863.

123

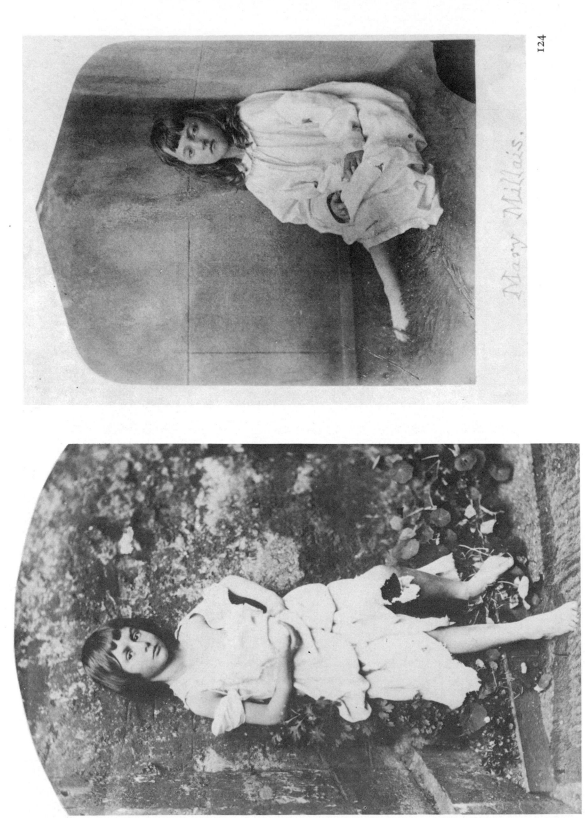

124

Mary Millais.

125

Lorina and Alice Liddell, daughters of the Dean of Ch. Ch.

126

124. LEWIS CARROLL. Mary Millais. 1865.
125. LEWIS CARROLL. Alice Liddell. *c.* 1860.
126. LEWIS CARROLL. Lorina and Alice Liddell. *c.* 1873.
127. LEWIS CARROLL. Thomas Woolner. 1860.

127

128

129

130

128. Stereoscope slide, Caernarvon Castle by FRANCIS
    BEDFORD. *c.* 1865.

129. Stereoscope slide. Photographer unknown. *c.* 1855.

130. Stereoscope slide, the Prussian Court at the 1862
    Exhibition by THE LONDON STEREOSCOPIC AND
    PHOTOGRAPHIC COMPANY.

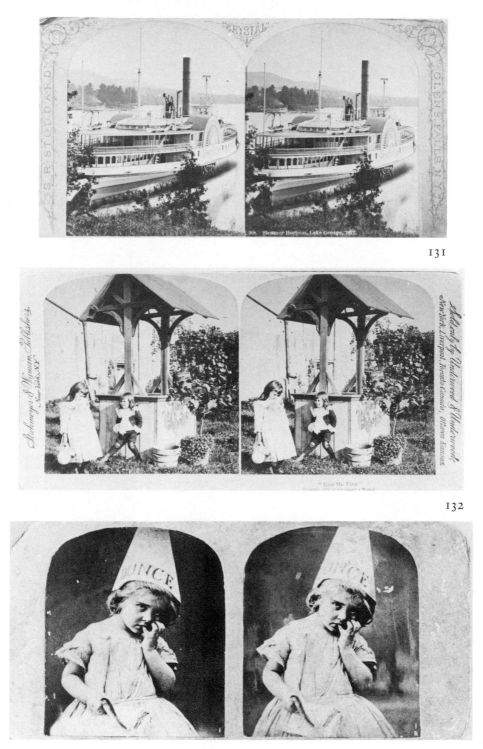

131. Stereoscope slide, the steamer *Horizon* on Lake George by S. R. STODDARD. 1877.

132. Stereoscope slide, 'Kiss Me First' by STROHMEYER and WYMAN. 1894.

133. Stereoscope slide. Photographer unknown. *c.* 1860.

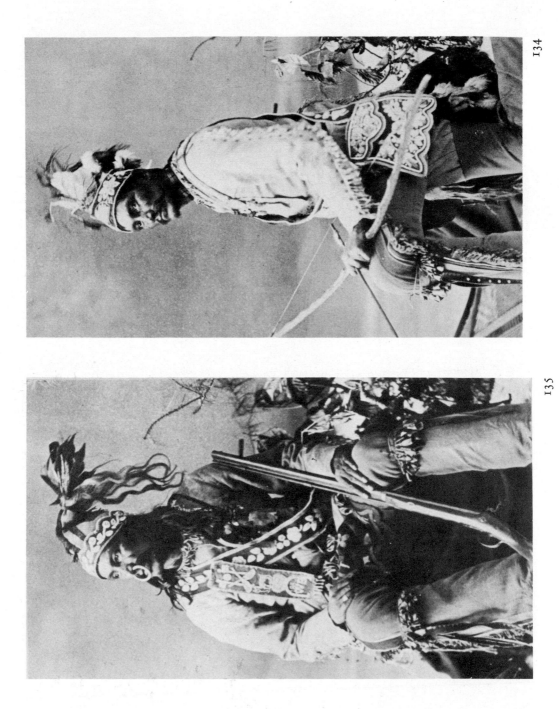

134

135

134, 135 and 136. WILLIAM NOTMAN. North American
Indians. *c.* 1875.

137. WILLIAM NOTMAN. The Halifax Commission.
1877.

136

137

138

138. TIMOTHY H. O'SULLIVAN. The Canyon of Chelly.
1873.
139. J. H. MAYBERRY. Miners at Bloody Gulch. *c.* 1880.
140. J. H. MAYBERRY. A cow puncher. *c.* 1880.

139

140

141

142

141. JAMES VALENTINE. Festiniog railway. *c.* 1880.

142. GEORGE WASHINGTON WILSON. Rievaulx Abbey. *c.* 1880.

143. GEORGE WASHINGTON WILSON. Abbotsford—the frontispiece to *The Poetical Works of Sir Walter Scott.* 1886.

144. HENRY DIXON. The Oxford Arms, Warwick Lane, London. 1875.

143

144

145

146

147

148

149

145. FREDERICK HOLLYER. Edward Burne-Jones and
William Morris. Platinotype. 1874.

146. FREDERICK HOLLYER. Camille Pissaro. Platinotype. *c.* 1895.

147. FREDERICK HOLLYER. Simeon Solomon. Platinotype. 1896.

148. FREDERICK HOLLYER. John Ruskin. Platinotype.
c. 1898.

149. FREDERICK HOLLYER. Alfred Gilbert. Platinotype.
1892.

150

151

150. CHARLES SOULIER. Le Château de Chillon. *c.* 1880.

151. CHARLES SOULIER. Panorama of Paris. *c.* 1880.

152. E. NEURDEIN. Sculpture in Amiens Cathedral. *c.* 1885.

152

153

154

155

156

153. BISSON FRÈRES. The Matterhorn. *c.* 1865.

154. J. JULLIEN. Chalets at Zermatt. *c.* 1885.

155. ETIENNE CARJAT. Victor Hugo. Woodburytype. 1877.

156. ANTOINE ADAM-SALOMON. Jules Verne. Woodburytype. 1877.

157. GIORGIO SOMMER. Sorrento. *c.* 1880.

157

158. Cabinet Portrait, by LAFAYETTE. *c.* 1880.
159. Cabinet Portrait, by JOSÉ MORA. *c.* 1880.
160. Cabinet Portrait, by TURNER and DRINKWATER. *c.* 1880.

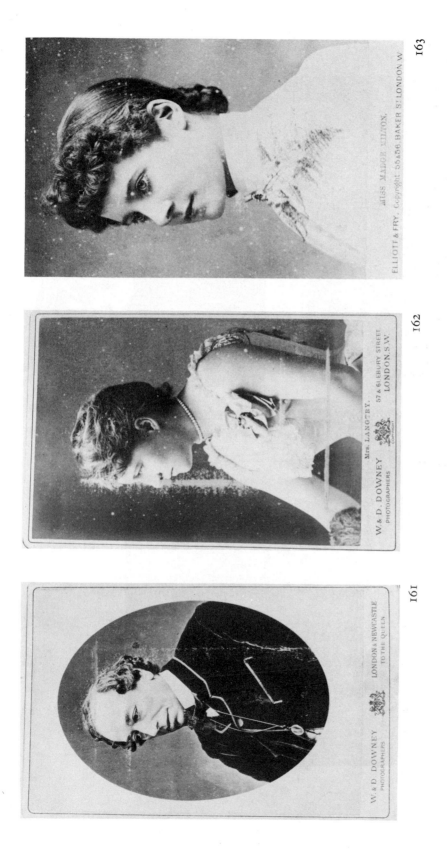

161. Cabinet Portrait, Benjamin Disraeli by W. and D. DOWNEY. c. 1875.

162. Cabinet Portrait, Lily Langtry by W. and D. DOWNEY. c. 1890.

163. Cabinet Portrait, Madge Milton by ELLIOTT and FRY. c. 1890.

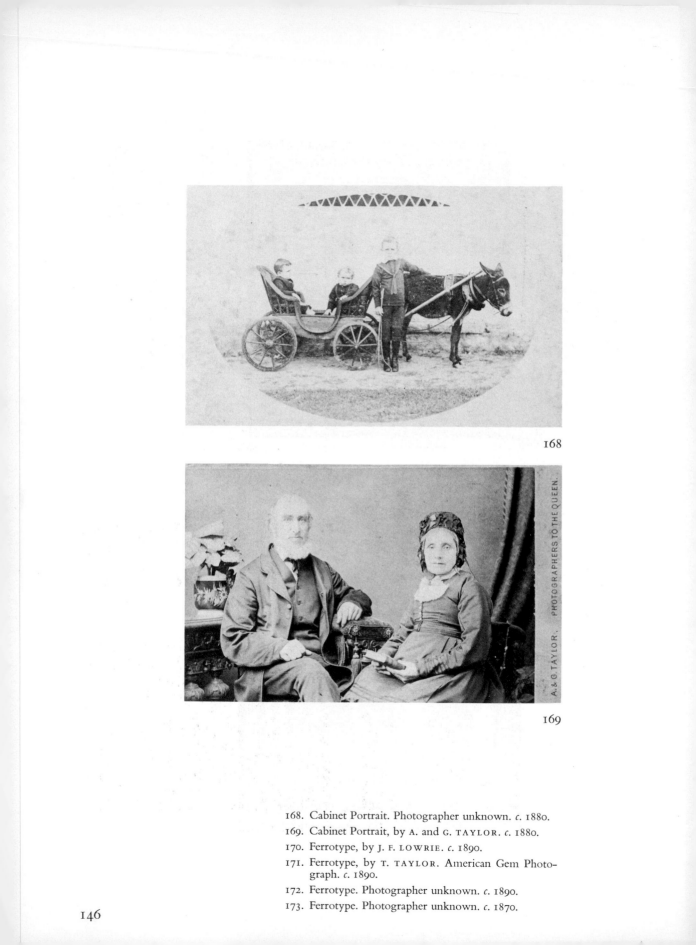

168

169

168. Cabinet Portrait. Photographer unknown. *c.* 1880.

169. Cabinet Portrait, by A. and G. TAYLOR. *c.* 1880.

170. Ferrotype, by J. F. LOWRIE. *c.* 1890.

171. Ferrotype, by T. TAYLOR. American Gem Photograph. *c.* 1890.

172. Ferrotype. Photographer unknown. *c.* 1890.

173. Ferrotype. Photographer unknown. *c.* 1870.

170

171

172

173

174

174, 175 and 176. EADWEARD MUYBRIDGE. Illustrations
for *Animal Locomotion*. Photogravures. 1887.

175

176

177

Panorama des Jetées du Havre

N. D. Phot

178

Photo. La Giraudon de Paris

177. E. NEURDEIN. Panorama des Jetées du Havre.
c. 1890.

178. E. NEURDEIN. La Colonnade du Louvre, Paris.
1889.

179. ETIENNE MAREY and GEORGES DEMENY. Illustration for *Étude de Physiologie Artistique. Des Mouvements de l'Homme.* 1893.

180. PAUL NADAR. Nadar père's interview with C. F.
Chevreul, aged 100. 1886.

181

182

181. J. POUNCY. The Down House Servants. *c.* 1875. (from a carte-de-visite).

182. GEORGE WASHINGTON WILSON. Windsor. *c.* 1880.

183. BENJAMIN STONE. Yeomen of the Guard at the Tower of London. 1898.

183

184

185

154

184. PAUL MARTIN. Billingsgate porters, London. 1894.

185. PAUL MARTIN. A street vendor, London. 1894.

186. PAUL MARTIN. Poor children in Lambeth, London.
1891/2.

186

187

188

187. PAUL MARTIN. Punch and Judy at Ilfracombe, Devon. 1894.

188. PAUL MARTIN. Paddlers at Yarmouth. 1892.

189. HUGHES and MULLINS. Queen Victoria. *c.* 1895.

190. FRANK BEKEN. The yacht *Suzanne*. 1910.

189

190

191

191. JAMES PATTISON. A sea-coal gatherer, Seaton
Carew, Durham. *c.* 1890.

192. JAMES PATTISON. Cockle gatherers, Seaton Carew,
Durham. *c.* 1890.

193. JAMES PATTISON. The lifeboat, Seaton Carew,
Durham. *c.* 1890.

192

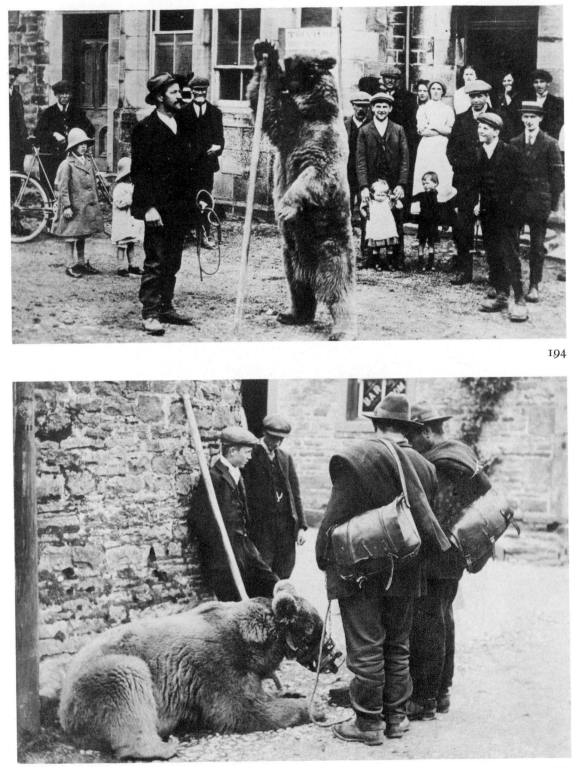

194

195

196

194 and 195. JAMES PATTISON. A dancing bear at
St. John's Chapel, Weardale. *c*. 1910.

196. JAMES PATTISON. Outside school. *c*. 1910.

197, 198, 199, 200, 201 and 202. Photographic post cards.
Photographers unknown. c. 1895 to 1914.

200

201

202

163

203

204

203 and 204. R. E. E. GELL. The Boer War. Spion's Kop.
January 1900.

205

205. JACOB A. RIIS. A New York tenement flat. *c.* 1910.
206. LEWIS W. HINE. A Carolina cotton mill. 1908.

206

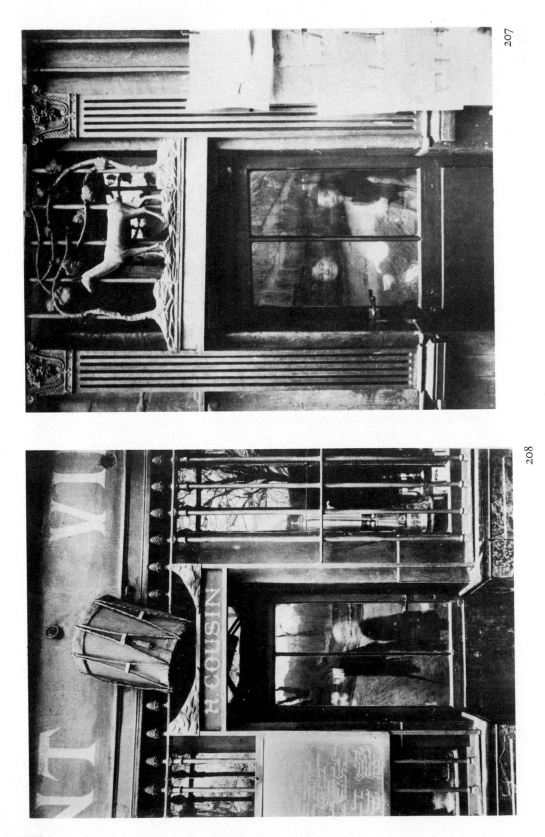

209

207, 208 and 209. EUGÈNE ATGET. Paris shop fronts and
signs. *c.* 1900.

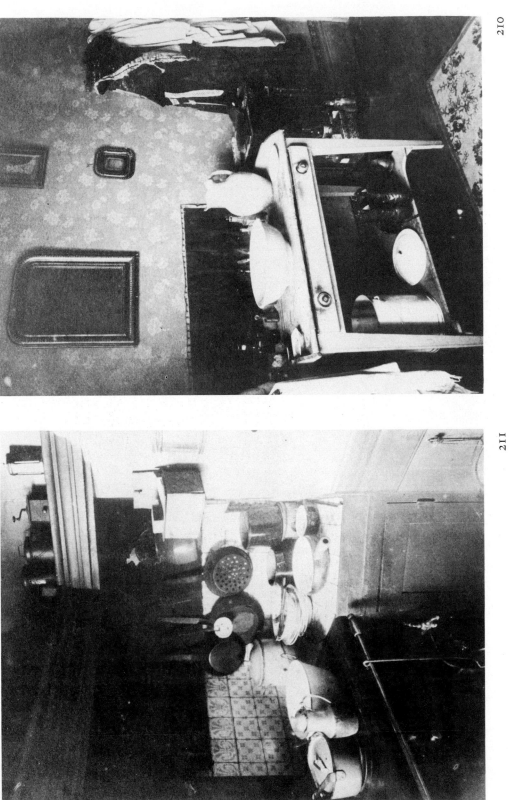

212

210, 211 and 212. EUGÈNE ATGET. Paris interiors.
c. 1910.

213

214

213 and 214. FRANK MEADOWS SUTCLIFFE. Yorkshire
genre. *c.* 1880/90.

215

216

215 and 216. FRANK MEADOWS SUTCLIFFE. Yorkshire
genre. c. 1880/90.

217

218

217. PETER HENRY EMERSON. The Waking River—
illustration for *Marsh Leaves*. 1885.

218. PETER HENRY EMERSON. A Winter's Sunrise—
illustration for *Marsh Leaves*. 1885.

219. PETER HENRY EMERSON. In the Barley Harvest.
Photogravure. *c.* 1890.

220. PETER HENRY EMERSON. Gathering Water-lilies.
Photogravure. 1886.

219

220

221

221. GEORGE DAVISON. The Onion Field. 1890. The
first impressionistic photograph.

222. BENJAMIN GAY WILKINSON. The Peaceful Evening
Hour. *c.* 1890.

222

223

223. ALFRED BALDRY and W. J. DAY. A Sea Frolic.
    c. 1895.
224. JOSEPH GALE. Homeward from the Plough. 1895.

224

225

226

227

225. JAMES CRAIG ANNAN. A Lombardy ploughing team. Photogravure. 1894.

226. ALEXANDER KEIGHLEY. Adieu.

227. A. HORSLEY HINTON. Day's Decline. 1895.

228

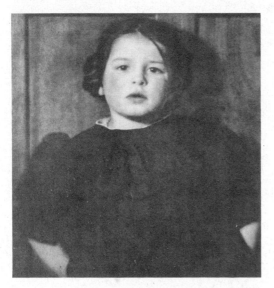

229

228. ROBERT DEMACHY. Nude. Gum print. *c.* 1898.

229. HEINRICH KÜHN. Portrait. *c.* 1900.

230. ROBERT DEMACHY. Au bord du Lac. Oil print.
     c. 1905.

231. HANS WATZEK. The White Sail. *c.* 1905.

230

231

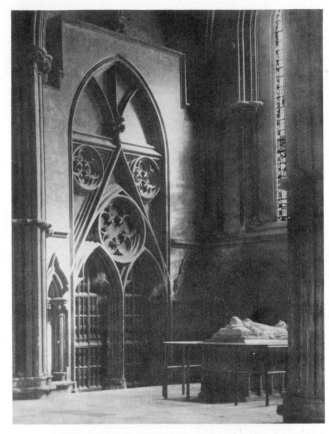

232

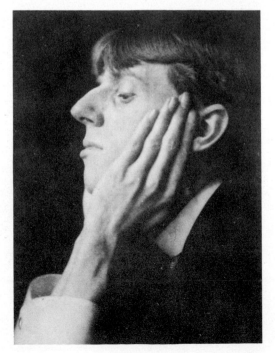

233

232. FREDERICK H. EVANS. In Sure and Certain Hope.
Platinotype. 1902.

233. FREDERICK H. EVANS. Aubrey Beardsley. c. 1893.

234. FREDERICK H. EVANS. Lincoln Cathedral. Platinotype. 1898.

234

235

236

235. C. PUYO. Portrait en Sanguine. Gum print. 1901.

236. THEODOR and OSKAR HOFMEISTER. The Hay-
maker. 1899.

237. LYDDELL SAWYER. Waiting for the Boats. c. 1899.

237

238

239

240

238. ALFRED STIEGLITZ. The Steerage. 1907.
239. ALFRED STIEGLITZ. Paris (2). *c.* 1900.
240. ALFRED STIEGLITZ. Winter, New York. 1892.

241

241. EDWARD STEICHEN. Auguste Rodin with his
sculptures of Victor Hugo and Le Penseur. Gum
print. 1902.

242. JAMES CRAIG ANNAN. Alvin Langdon Coburn.
c. 1906.

243. GERTRUDE KÄSEBIER. *The Sketch*. 1904.

242

243

244. ALVIN LANGDON COBURN. Regent's Canal, London. Photogravure. c. 1908.

245. ALVIN LANGDON COBURN. Tower Bridge, London. Photogravure. c. 1908.

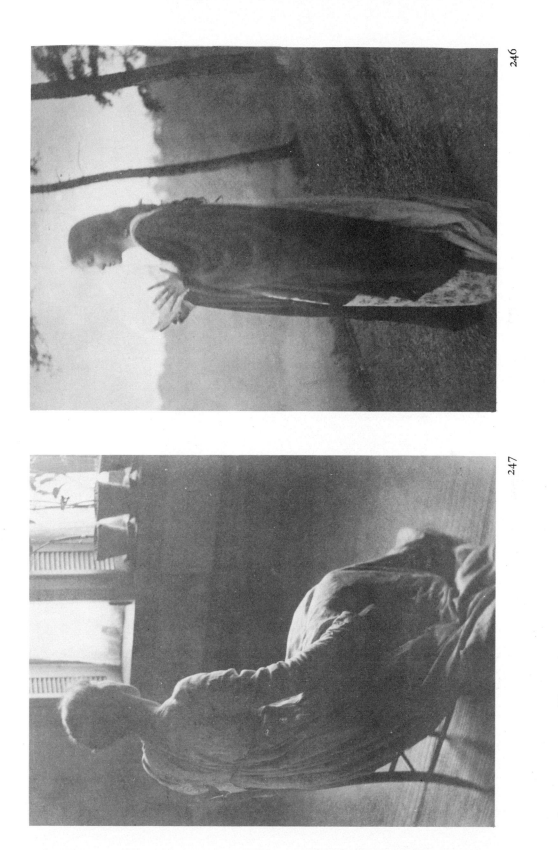

246

247

246. CLARENCE WHITE. The Watcher. 1906.
247. CLARENCE WHITE. Interior with figure. 1899.

248

248. FREDERICK HOLLAND DAY. The Crucifixion. 1898.
249. FREDERICK HOLLAND DAY. Torso. *c*. 1908.
250. FREDERICK HOLLAND DAY. The Vision. 1907.

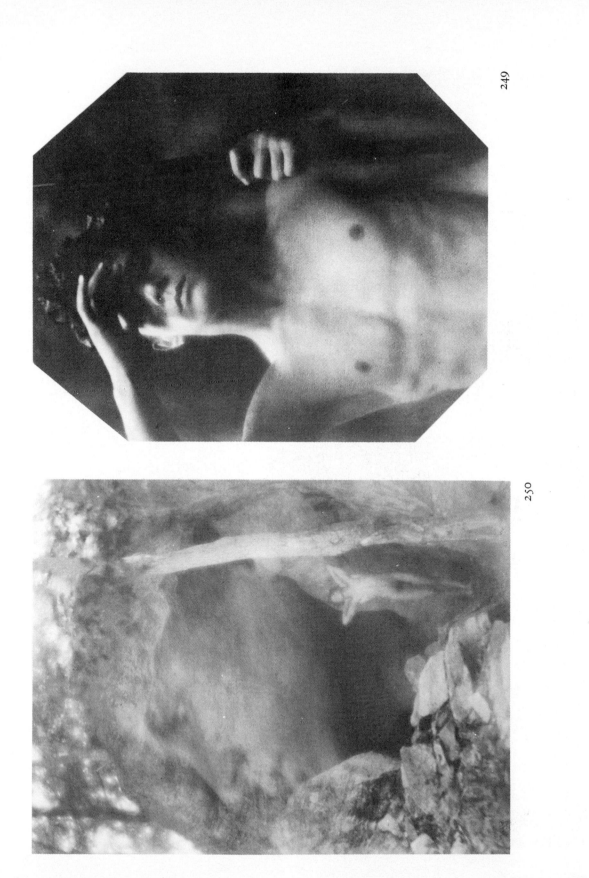

249

250

251. E. O. HOPPÉ. Prince Regent of Bavaria. Platinotype. 1909.

252. RICHARD POLAK. The Little Golfplayer. 1913.

251

252

Index

Numbers in heavy type refer to the main entries; numbers in italics to the illustrations.

SOMMER, Giorgio (G. SOMMER and FIGLIO): **38**, 61, *157*

SOULIER, Charles: 19, **38**, *150, 151*

SOUTHWORTH, Albert Sands (SOUTHWORTH and HAWES): **38**

SPENCER, J. B.: 30

de ST. CROIX, M.: **38**, 61

STEICHEN, Edward: **38**, **39**, 53, *241*

STELZNER, Carl Ferdinand: 10, **39**

STEPHENS, John Lloyd: 12, **39**

STEREOSCOPE: 4, 43, **53**, **54**, 57

STEWART, John: **39**

STIEGLITZ, Alfred: 39, **39**, 53, *238, 239, 240*

STODDARD, S. R.: **39**, *131*

STONE, Benjamin: **39**, *183*

STROHMEYER, –. (STROHMEYER and WYMAN): **39**, **40**, *132*

SUBTRACTIVE SYSTEM: 5, 17, 48

SUTCLIFFE, Frank Meadows: **40**, 53, 61, *80, 213, 214, 215, 216*

SWAN, Joseph Wilson: 5, **40**, 47

SYRUPED COLLODION PROCESS: **51**

TABER, I. W.: **40**

TALBOT, William Henry Fox: 1, 2, 3, 4, 13, 21, **40**, **41**, 46, 47, 49, 52, 55, 62, *11, 12, 13, 14, 15, 16*

TALBOTYPE: 2, 4, **40**, **46**

TAMOTO, K.: **40**, *94*

TANNIN PROCESS: 4, 36, **54**

TAYLOR, A. and G.: **41**, *164, 165, 169*

TAYLOR, T.: **41**, *171*

TENNYSON: 12, 59

THOMPSON, C. Thurston: **41**, 49

THOMPSON, S.: **41**, 56

THOMPSON, –.: 10

THOMSON, John: **41**, 62, *118, 119*

THOMSON, John (ROSS and THOMSON): 36

TINTYPE: 4, 29, **50**

TOURNACHON, Gaspard Félix: 31

TURNER, Benjamin Bracknell: **41**

TURNER, –. (TURNER and DRINKWATER): **41**, *160*

UENO, Toshinojo: **41**

UNDERWOOD, –. (UNDERWOOD and UNDERWOOD): **41**, **42**, 54

VACQUERIE, Auguste: 23

VALENTINE, James: **42**, 62, *141*

de VILLENEUVE, Julien Vallou: **42**, *27, 28, 29*

da VINCI, Leonardo: 1

VOIGTLÄNDER, Peter Wilhelm Friedrich: **42**

VORTOGRAPH: 13

WALKER, Samuel A.: **42**

WALKER, S. L.: **42**, 62

WALL, Edward John: 5, 34, **42**, 46

WALLER, J.: **42**

WATKINS, Carleton E.: **42**

WATKINS, Herbert: **42**

WATZEK, Hans: **42**, **43**, *231*

WAXED PAPER PROCESS: 4, 26, **54**

WEDGWOOD, Thomas: 1, 4

WET PLATE or WET COLLODION PROCESS: 4, 7, 46, 50, 51, 54, **54**

WHEATSTONE, Charles: 4, **43**, 53

WHITE, Clarence Hudson: **43**, *246, 247*

WHITE, Henry: **43**

WILKINSON, Benjamin Gay: **43**, *222*

WILLIS, William: 5, **43**, 52

WILSON, Charles A.: **43**

WILSON, George Washington: 15, 43, **43**, 54, 62, *142, 143, 182*

WOLCOTT, Alexander S.: 4, 24, **43**

WOODBURY, Francis (WOODBURY and PAGE): **44**

WOODBURY, Walter Bentley: 5, **44**, 54

WOODBURYTYPE: 5, **44**, **54**

WRIGGLESWORTH, –. (WRIGGLESWORTH and BINNS): **44**

WYMAN, –. (STROHMEYER and WYMAN): **39**, **40**, *132*

WYNFIELD, David Wilkie: **44**

ZAMBRA, Joseph (NEGRETTI and ZAMBRA): **31**, **32**, 44, *91, 92*